China Ink

The Changing Face
of Chinese Journalism

Judy Polumbaum
with Xiong Lei

Illustrations by Margaret Kearney

ROWMAN & LITTLEFIELD PUBLISHERS, INC.
Lanham • Boulder • New York • Toronto • Plymouth, UK

ROWMAN & LITTLEFIELD PUBLISHERS, INC.

Published in the United States of America
by Rowman & Littlefield Publishers, Inc.
A wholly owned subsidary of The Rowman & Littlefield Publishing Group, Inc.
4501 Forbes Boulevard, Suite 200, Lanham, Maryland 20706
www.rowmanlittlefield.com

Estover Road, Plymouth PL6 7PY, United Kingdom

Copyright © 2008 by Judy Polumbaum
All drawings by Margaret Kearney.

British Library Cataloguing in Publication Information Available

Library of Congress Cataloging-in-Publication Data

China ink : the changing face of Chinese journalism / [edited by] Judy Polumbaum with
Xiong Lei.
    p. cm. -- (Asian voices)
  Includes index.
  ISBN-13: 978-0-7425-5667-6 (cloth : alk. paper)
  ISBN-10: 0-7425-5667-0 (cloth : alk. paper)
  ISBN-13: 978-0-7425-5668-3 (pbk. : alk. paper)
  ISBN-10: 0-7425-5668-9 (pbk. : alk. paper)
  1. Journalists--China--Interviews. 2. Journalism--China. I. Polumbaum, Judy. II. Xiong,
Lei.
  PN5366.A315C45 2008
  0079'.51--dc22
                                    2008002126

Printed in the United States of America

⊗ ™ The paper used in this publication meets the minimum requirements of American
National Standard for Information Sciences—Permanence of Paper for Printed Library
Materials, ANSI/NISO Z39.48-1992.

China Ink

ASIAN VOICES
A Subseries of Asian/Pacific/Perspectives
Series Editor: Mark Selden

To our fathers:

Ted Polumbaum (1924–2001)
&
Xiong Xianghui (1919–2005)

Contents

Part II: Into the Fray

Part III: In the Niches

Part IV: Over the Air

Part V: New Configurations

Foreword

Aryeh Neier
President, Open Society Institute

*T*here is, of course, a vast literature about freedom struggles in different parts of the world, but it is difficult to find much that has been written about the part played by the factor that has become most significant in contemporary China: professionalism. It is professionalism that seems to drive some Chinese lawyers to represent their clients in ways that challenge the authority of state officials. It is professionalism that inspires some Chinese physicians to address previously unmentionable matters such as drug addiction and the HIV/AIDS epidemic, and that forced the shift in 2003 from cover-up of SARS and a potential public health disaster to full disclosure, cooperation with the World Health Organization, and success in controlling the disease. And it is professionalism that seems to make some Chinese journalists dig deep and pursue stories that may embarrass some of those who wield power.

Because China is so vast, there are probably hundreds of thousands of journalists in the country. No doubt the majority, as any place else, do their jobs perfunctorily. But among them there are certainly hundreds and there are probably thousands who are sufficiently imbued with the spirit of professionalism so that they do not just repeat the information provided to them; they look for ways to check its accuracy and to pursue sides of the story that may be neglected; or they may themselves take the initiative in developing stories. Environmental issues, labor difficulties, health problems, land disputes, abuses of power, and corruption are among the issues that are being covered today meaningfully in the Chinese media.

There are limits, of course. The Chinese journalists I have encountered seem to have a well-developed sense of how far they can go. Indeed, the English language material I have seen on one Chinese magazine says: "We know where the line is and we go right up to it." Inevitably, because the line shifts and its placement may vary depending on a range of factors, some journalists get into trouble. Yet despite the risks they run and occasional setbacks, the professionalism of Chinese journalists is gradually expanding the space in which they are able to operate. This is the process by which their professionalism, and the professionalism of some of their counterparts in other lines of work, is expanding freedom in China. It is a slow process, but it has already accomplished a lot. The interviews published here provide a unique opportunity for readers to gain insights into a distinctive and largely unheralded freedom struggle that seems to me as important as any in our time.

New York City
November 2007

Introduction

Judy Polumbaum

The trend we call globalization, characterized and propelled by accelerating flows of people, money, information, and ideas among countries, would seem to have vastly expanded the means for people in disparate parts of the world to understand each other. Quite apart from debates over the dislocations, imbalances, and tensions the process generates, globalization surely has introduced ample opportunities for reciprocal learning across cultures. This ought to be the case for Americans and Chinese, whose exchanges via tourism, education, commerce, science, sports, and the arts continue to grow exponentially. Knowledge about the complexities of Chinese society is widely available to those who seek it: International scholars have more access than ever, and major news outlets have capable and sophisticated correspondents on the ground.

Yet simplistic, outmoded stereotypes about China and Chinese people—yellow peril, red menace, blue ant—somehow maintain traction in the U.S. imagination. Scratch the surface, and one finds that even educated Americans construe Chinese culture as inscrutable, China's political system as totalistic, Chinese citizens as robotic. The first-time visitor to China may be surprised to find that the ostensibly totalitarian machinery operates inexactly and often unpredictably, while the ranks of the presumably cowed masses boast their share of steadfast nonconformists, insouciant characters, and irreverent wags. Not just to the naïve, but to those who should know better, the realization that the land of exotica is peopled with ordinary flesh-and-blood human beings going about their daily lives may come as an epiphany.

Presumptions of a controlled, mechanistic system are all the more entrenched in conceptions of the news media. The skeptical or probing journalist is taken as the exception; the "dissident" who challenges the system is upheld as the brave alternative. One Chinese journalistic troublemaker lauded in U.S.

media accounts in recent years, Li Datong, who was removed as editor of a newspaper supplement for running articles that irked propaganda authorities, begs to differ. Foreigners "mistakenly imagine that all Chinese journalists are meek, obedient and living in fear," Li told radio journalist Anthony Kuhn, "but we're not."[1]

Li Datong may be bolder than others in going public with his objections to propaganda dictates, but criticism and frank talk are not hard to find in Chinese press circles. This collection of interviews with reporters and editors who have entered the field in the last two decades is testimony to the independence, determination, and energies of younger generations of Chinese journalists. Our conversations with these men and women reveal a diversity, passion, humor, and optimism that belie stereotypes of cogs in the machine. The context in which they work—language, cultural traditions, political constraints—remains quite different from that of most Western journalists; yet increasingly they confront concerns and problems that will sound familiar to reporters and editors elsewhere, from bottom-line pressures to sheer exhaustion. And perhaps it's inevitable that, the more they speak and the more carefully we listen, the better we come to appreciate their circumstances, motivations, and aspirations.

My longtime friend and colleague Xiong Lei, an accomplished journalist in her own right, joined me in planning and conducting these interviews. I'd been tracking developments in Chinese journalism since the late 1970s as a visiting teacher and researcher; in 1987–1988, as a doctoral student and beneficiary of growing academic exchange, I was one of the first Western media scholars permitted to do bona fide fieldwork in China. It used to be that friends and associates would alert me to noteworthy stories, incidents, and discussions in the field; now the Internet performs much of that grapevine role, and astute bloggers with interest in Chinese media make it even easier to follow affairs from abroad. Nevertheless, each time I returned to China, on intermittent visits ranging from a few weeks to a semester, I felt events outpacing me yet again. Finally, I proposed to Xiong Lei that we sit down with a sampling of young journalists and, in a concerted manner, hear them out on thoughts and practices likely to help shape journalism in the coming years. Good-naturedly, she agreed; the project evidently gave her license to refer to me ever after as a slave driver. In truth, we both found the excursion fun and illuminating beyond our expectations.

Our subjects, ranging in age from early twenties to early forties, come from a variety of news organizations, including established official organs of the Chinese Communist Party and government and newer commercial upstarts. Most are print journalists (the "ink" of our title handily references the ascendancy of the marketplace as well), a few are in broadcasting, and virtually all are doing work that feeds into the Internet. Some we knew by reputation;

others were introduced through personal or collegial networks as examples of energetic, enterprising, thoughtful young journalists. All were based in Beijing at the times we conversed, although many do a good deal of reporting in other parts of the country, several have reported from abroad, and a few have had study opportunities overseas. A handful have changed jobs since we talked, which we indicate in introductions to each account, although none has entirely left the field.

Our conversations took place in Beijing hotel rooms, lobbies, teashops, and offices at various times from late 2005 through late 2006, and were conducted in Mandarin Chinese, sometimes sprinkled with English or "Chinglish." The interviews have been transcribed, translated, and edited in the fashion popularized by oral historian Studs Terkel—true to the original words, with some rearrangement for the sake of narrative flow and coherence.[2] And insofar as one can convey attitude and voice in translation, I have endeavored to do so.

We deliberately did not seek out journalists who have broken with the system and earned the label of "dissident." Challenging the legitimacy of the ruling party in public forums is an obvious way to court surveillance, detention, and prison. But in China today, such methods do not attract large constituencies, and their international repercussions produce little domestic leverage. Some dissidents have been pressured into exile, only to find themselves ineffectual; the starkest example from China's old guard of investigative reporters is the late Liu Bingyuan, still admired by those who knew his work but sadly out of touch with a changing China when he died in New Jersey in December 2005. Other dissidents in exile have proven susceptible to blandishments from overtly anti-Beijing or pro-Taiwan groups, or have followed opportunities to build new careers and make money abroad.

In short, dissidents may be brave, or foolhardy, or laudable, or fickle; but it would be a mistake to regard them as an especially influential force for democratic change within China, let alone as the sole standard-bearers for freedom of information and expression. None of the journalists we interviewed for this project work through oppositional channels—which, as any one of them will acknowledge, are simply not allowed in China. However, neither is this an exercise in showing how well the system works.

For that matter, neither do our findings bode especially well for China's emulation of Western market-driven models. From George Seldes's *Lords of the Press* to Ben Bagdikian's *The Media Monopoly* to Robert McChesney's *Rich Media, Poor Democracy*, U.S. media critics and scholars have long decried the dangers that corporate domination of media poses to serious journalism.[3] With further corporate consolidation, shrinking news budgets, blurring of news and entertainment, and multiplying entanglements among media, money, and politics, alarm on the part of news practitioners in the land of the First Amendment has only grown.[4] Article 35 of the Chinese Constitution promises freedom of speech and the press for Chinese citizens; and as China hurtles headlong down a path of what surely looks like capitalism, with its often rapacious consequences, albeit in the name of "socialism with Chinese characteristics," some of the same concerns about market threats to such ideals are emerging in China as well.

It is logical that the Chinese intelligentsia, among whom journalists count themselves, would be articulating these concerns. China's intellectuals have inherited a tradition of loyal opposition and forthright criticism. Like intellectuals anywhere, they also are known to brood and complain. At the same time, even the most modern of Chinese carry the burden of upholding their whole nation's reputation (or maintaining collective as well as individual "face"). Some are reticent to air what they consider insider problems. Others are simply too preoccupied with the practical stresses of modern life to dwell on big philosophical questions. Nevertheless, most of the twenty journalists we interviewed talked frankly about the challenges they face in trying to do meaningful journalism within a propagandistic tradition, under state controls, and in the context of rampant commercialization. They provided ample examples of persistence, enterprise, and boldness in efforts to gain access to news sites and sources, determination in persuading editors of the importance of their stories, and responsiveness to results of publication or broadcast.

We posed similar questions to all our interviewees, asking them to relate how they entered the field, their foremost principles for journalism, gratifications and difficulties they face in their work, accomplishments of which they are proudest, and expectations for developments in Chinese media in the coming decade. Perhaps the most striking aspect of our interviews is the variety of responses—there is no single way of becoming or "being" a journalist in China today. Some majored in journalism at college or graduate school; others took roundabout paths, in some cases veering sharply from earlier career plans. Work methods and arrangements vary greatly; some of these journalists have comfortable sinecures while others work for piece rates. Some find satisfaction in small daily achievements; others seek fulfillment in writing books. Some take great pride in commendations from national leaders for constructive reporting on complex issues; others find glee in being a thorn in the side of officials. The challenges that seem to loom largest may be as mundane as limits of time or space; they may be organizational, related to operation of editorial hierarchies; they may be structural, stemming from dictates of central or local propaganda authorities; more often they are a combination.

Commonalities also emerge. The most reflective journalists have strong social consciousness and ethical awareness. They favor fact over preconception. They believe in compassion and sensitivity. They pick their battles, negotiating strategically with sources, editors, and officials in the interests of illuminating important public issues and drawing attention to problems. They are perturbed by the commercial imperatives seeping into news endeavors, while seeing this trend as inexorable in China's current climate of profit seeking. Most like their work for its intrinsic rewards and the sense of having a ringside seat at key rounds of history; they are not averse to making names for themselves, but don't necessarily expect to.

The tenor of the criticism journalists offer these days has changed markedly since an earlier period of considerable ferment and discussion in the field, during the late 1980s, when I did my dissertation research.[5] Back then, journalists complained most emphatically about restrictions on their autonomy, with an emphasis on external constraints. Today, the mood is self-questioning. Journalists ponder how to avail themselves of opportunities for doing good work. Rather than belaboring how the system holds them back, the individuals we interviewed were more likely to speak of their own shortcomings. Most had a sense of urgency about the need to develop knowledge, improve skills, and raise standards of professionalism.

The question will arise as to whether our subjects were being candid with us. Indeed, a few obviously wished to avoid touchy areas. Not surprisingly, those offering the most positive gloss on the news business were least inclined to let even the mildest reservation emerge in the final edited transcripts of our conversations. Invited to review their comments for publication, most of our interviewees requested no revisions, although a few supplied minor factual corrections. We could have predicted the two or three who might have had second thoughts, and, indeed, the most reserved individuals excised what we saw as fairly innocuous statements.

Someone reluctant to answer a question usually said so in the first place, which itself could be a revealing response. Occasionally someone would go "off the record," and we have respected these confidences. More often than not, however, something one person had reservations about discussing turned out to be precisely what another wanted to discuss openly at length. Given that one of the interviewers has worked in the Chinese media for a quarter-century and the other has studied journalism in contemporary China for as long, we would like to think we could discern dissimulation. More important, though, is the fact that the majority of our interviewees were forthcoming about difficulties and dilemmas as well as achievements and satisfactions—even more so than in the late 1980s, with all its outspokenness and raging debates. The results are good indicators, we believe, of overall tendencies and trends in Chinese news work.

Other questions come up as well. Is it a conflict of interest for a reporter to be a government representative? Gong Wen, economics reporter for the

People's Daily, accompanied China's official delegation to World Trade Organization deliberations; she speaks as the only journalist accorded front-row exclusives as well as access to confidential information she could not disclose. As a staffer for the official paper of the Chinese Communist Party, China's governing party by law, Gong Wen is among the most official of the official. This does not mean passively transmitting unexamined messages, however; she sees her role as actively gathering data and making independent analyses. Meanwhile, we must acknowledge the environment in which she works. Nowhere in the world do media operate outside the realms of prevailing political and economic systems. China has no such thing as media truly independent from the state—only degrees of independence, which vary greatly across time, place, and situation and, depending on circumstances and personalities, can be leveraged into greater opportunities.

What should we make of journalists serving the mission of government-sponsored media designed to promote "harmony" among China's dozens of ethnic groups? This happens to be part of the mosaic of what the Chinese consider journalism, and a reminder that conventions differ across cultures and systems. Yang Jin, reporter and editor for a national magazine on minority affairs, and of Tibetan ethnicity herself, seems comfortable with her publication's mission, neither questioning nor defensive of its premises. Outsiders' assumptions may be rather irrelevant to how insiders view their work.

Certainly, reporters for high-level national media organs are keenly attuned to propaganda priorities and proscriptions. U.S. scholar Ashley Esarey's detailed examination of Party monitoring of the media, personnel powers, legal and extra-legal restrictions, and incentives to encourage compliance covers the territory well.[6] Some journalists are matter-of-fact about working within this structure; others suggest the Chinese government is simply more open about its propaganda designs than other governments; a few—often Party members themselves—scoff or poke fun at the propaganda arbiters; some sound restrained or reticent when discussing the media managers; none welcome their interventions.

Yet the bounds of state control are far more elastic than formal lines of authority and rules of supervision might suggest, and journalists are constantly testing the parameters, sometimes brashly, more often in subtle ways. Surprising as it might seem, but understandable in light of China's vast territory and population, the media control system relies largely on vague guidelines, changeable instructions, and responses after the fact, rather than on rigid prepublication censorship. In the absence of specific orders or mechanisms preventing reporting, some journalists are willing to tread into sensitive areas and brook post-hoc criticism, or even job reassignments.

Audacity is always a gamble, of course; groundbreaking reporting may be accepted and even praised, or the bearer of an unwelcome message may find himself relieved of his beat and consigned to obscure tasks. Li Datong, for instance, the editor quoted earlier, was sidelined to a research office. At the same time, he has remained engaged with public affairs, and English translations of his commentaries regularly appear on the Internet via the openDemocracy website, a U.K.-based not-for-profit forum on global affairs. One of our interviewees, investigative reporter Liu Jianqiang, found himself out of a job after figuring in a front-page story in a major Western newspaper. Yet he continued to do valuable work, including writing under pennames; and when top leadership at his own paper churned yet again, he was welcomed back.

Political missteps are not the only trigger for trouble; media outlets sometimes get shut down in sweeps to eliminate pornography or shady operations, or for managerial or budgetary glitches that just happen to hit the radar of administrative bureaucracies. Of course, political transgressions get more attention than bureaucratic technicalities—on occasion prompting replacement of an entire leadership tier, and less often causing organizational fatalities. The paper *21st Century World Herald*, begun in 2001 with a focus on international news, took a few too many risks and was closed two years later. Meanwhile, a sister startup with a business focus, *21st Century World Economic Herald*, which also takes risks, is still going strong; founding editor Liu Zhouwei is among our interviewees.

Nowadays, transgressions seldom result in imprisonment, compel exile, or end careers. The expansion of China's media marketplace and growth of the publishing industry have created new opportunities and outlets for projects on controversial subjects and more fluidity in the workforce. Wang Jun, an urban affairs reporter who implicated Beijing leaders in questionable real estate dealings, subsequently was transferred from a daily news bureau to a weekly magazine, where he has greater latitude and less pressure. He expressed amazement at the acclaim he received for his book chronicling mishaps in Beijing's city planning over the decades, and cheerfully entertained the notion that if he lost his journalism job he could survive by writing books. Photojournalist and editor Jin Yongquan, who also works on books, was similarly surprised at a publisher's readiness to take on his book about the displacement of entire villages by the giant Three Gorges dam project, and thinks perhaps journalists inhibit themselves by overestimating pitfalls that may await them.

Considerable debate revolves around the phenomenon of commercialization, with media practitioners finding both good and bad in the market mentality. Responsiveness to readers can also mean pandering to popular taste for sensationalism. Competition can lead to shortcuts and slipshod work. While those we interviewed take pride in their own concern for accuracy, many feel shoddy practices have undermined the credibility of news organizations generally, and that respect for journalists has declined as a result. To younger journalists, vexations generated by commercialism may have more direct salience than political imperatives or impediments. Hu Zhibin, as a cub reporter for the newspaper *The First*, which emphasizes sports and lifestyle, felt driven more by the dictates of the market's appetite for stories than by Party or government demands. He, too, expressed frustration at officials keeping information under wraps—but what American reporter has ever found openness to be the hall-mark of officialdom?

To what extent should a journalist be a moral educator? This in part is the role Xiang Fei has assumed as a late-night radio host. Xiang seems driven to help people make socially appropriate decisions as a route to personal happi-ness. She prefaced her account of persuading a fugitive criminal to turn himself in by telling us the saga was "very Chinese"; indeed, China's cultural traditions and political habits have long emphasized moral obligation. But how Chinese is this sort of mission, really? Possibly U.S. talk show hosts are no less moral crusaders, albeit in the guise of entertainment personalities. And news accounts in all societies, implicitly if not overtly, often set up moral exemplars and make judgments about good and bad.

In fact, for all its distinctiveness, Chinese journalism is not the antithesis one might expect to the journalism I know best: that produced by the United States. Throughout this project, the shortcomings, paradoxes, and contradic-tions of my own system have never been far from my mind. Media's capac-ity to foster the dissemination of information and ideas deserves celebration when it works, but forces of inhibition, manipulation, and distortion—be they outgrowths of the marketplace, flaws of the political system, or exacerbations of war, fear, and insecurity—cannot be ignored. In China, the challenges may take different and often more intimidating forms, but the categories are similar, ranging from economic imperatives, political projects, cultural assumptions, and ideological blinders to the power of convention, habit, and routine. More-over, as China shifts from a centrally planned to a market-driven economy, and as a once-coherent ideology gives way to pluralistic thinking, the parallels seem ever more evident.

So, in the pages that follow, meet twenty individuals with as many ways of looking at their vocations and work environments, the larger society, and the world. Some work for established national media outlets with enduring propa-ganda missions; counterintuitively, these strongholds already are saturated with an ethos of professionalism. Others work in market-oriented startups, or at niche media in specialized areas such as sports and science, or in broadcasting. A final section presents individuals present at the creation of their organizations and in positions that give them an overview.

An obvious omission is the ever-expanding arena of web journalism. Journalists in traditional broadcast and print outlets invariably participate in increasingly important web extensions of their mediums; and some of our in-terviewees, including Zhou Yijun, Lu Yi, Ma Yin, and Zhang Lixian, are active bloggers. However, this round of interviews does not include journalists whose work is primarily or exclusively web-based. That easily is another book.

None of our interviewees finds his or her job easy, nor do they seem the sort to take an easy route if one existed. All feel lucky to be in an endlessly interesting line of work, in a practice that puts them in fascinating situations and teaches them more than one can learn from theory or books, although they deem thinking and reading precious pursuits as well. Even when they are scrambling, they have a sense of history and progress. Even while sharing woes, they emanate optimism and fortitude. The nitty-gritty of their jobs might tire them out but doesn't grind them down; where the present seems confusing or dismaying, they take a long view. Ultimately, the adventure of trying to make sense of dynamic and often bewildering times is an honor, a privilege, a mission, and its own reward. Their outlook surely will resonate with Western journalists who feel beleaguered, weary, and underappreciated, yet nonetheless relish going into battle each day.

These are people we feel fortunate to have spent time with and learned from. We do not deem them paragons, models, or archetypes. Nor do we claim they are representative of Chinese journalists overall; in fact, they are atypi-cal in some respects. Although the field in general draws personnel from the college-educated, this group includes a disproportion with elite educational backgrounds. Our interviewees have cosmopolitan outlooks fostered by living and working in the country's political center, and more access to international contacts than their counterparts in smaller cities or in China's interior.

Instead, we see these individuals as harbingers of trends and tendencies in Chinese journalism and intellectual life. Their experiences and ideas trace the boundaries that circumscribe what is possible in news work; their satisfactions and aspirations illuminate achievements attained and prospects yet to be real-ized. They've given us a tour of the terrain in times of transition, bringing to the surface contradictions and quandaries faced by Chinese intellectuals during a period of dizzying change.

This collection highlights, we believe, the myriad ways individuals think about and carry out their work and try to make a difference. And it offers, we hope, a corrective to views of Chinese public life as monolithically controlled by the state—an impression that, despite two decades of research suggesting otherwise, continues to pervade American media accounts and influence U.S. public opinion and policy. Our project also shows, however, that the develop-ment of freedom of information and expression in China entails struggles at multiple levels, and that political liberalization is by no means an automatic outcome of economic liberalization.

Above all, we hope these conversations will contribute to broadening popular understandings of China—and, of course, to continuing conversations.

NOTES

1. National Public Radio, "Morning Edition," 7 March 2006.
2. Terkel's best-known work in this vein is *Working: People Talk About What They Do All Day and How They Feel About What They Do* (New York: Pantheon, 1974).
3. The tradition includes, for starters: George Seldes, *Lords of the Press* (New York: J. Messner, 1938); Commission on Freedom of the Press, *A Free and Responsible Press* (University of Chicago Press, 1947); A. J. Liebling, *The Press* (New York: Ballantine, 1964); Noam Chomsky, *Necessary Illusions: Thought Control in Democratic Societies* (Boston: South End Press, 1989); Ben Bagdikian, *The New Media Monopoly* (Boston: Beacon, 2004); Robert McChesney, *Rich Media, Poor Democracy: Communication Politics in Dubious Times* (Urbana: University of Illinois Press, 1999).
4. See, for instance, Bill Kovach and Tom Rosenstiel, *The Elements of Journalism: What Newspeople Should Know and the Public Should Expect* (New York: Crown, 2001); Leonard Downie and Robert Kaiser, *The News About the News: American Journalism in Peril* (New York: Vintage, 2003); Howard Gardner, Mihaly Csikszentmihalyi & William Damon, *Good Work: When Excellence & Ethics Meet* (New York: Basic, 2002).
5. On this period, see Chin-chuan Lee, ed., *Voices of China: The Interplay of Politics and Journalism* (New York: Guilford, 1990), including my chapter, "The Tribulations of China's Journalists after a Decade of Reform," 33–68.
6. *Speak No Evil: Mass Media Control in Contemporary China* (Washington, DC: Freedom House, February 2006).

I

THE CHANGING ESTABLISHMENT

Wang Jun
王军

Outlook Weekly
了望周刊

$\mathcal{W}$ang Jun takes a long view of contemporary affairs. As a reporter for Xinhua News Agency, he covered Beijing's urban construction boom, and in the process became an expert on city planning—and the ruinous effects of lack of planning. He is fiercely committed to journalism as a project of witness and documentation. At the same time, he has a spirited sense of the ridiculous. His interview transcript begins with this sound check:

> Q: What's your name?
> A: Wang Jun.
> Q: How old are you?
> A: It's a secret!

Xinhua—which means "new China"—is the behemoth of Chinese news organizations, with bureaus across China and worldwide. The organization has multiple and sometimes contradictory purposes. Long considered the authoritative voice of the Chinese government, it also strives for the global credibility of a Reuters or Associated Press. Xinhua increasingly seeks commercial viability as well. Wang Jun now writes and edits at one of its most popular ancillary publications, *Outlook Weekly*, while also working on books and mentoring younger colleagues. He was born in April 1969. We talked in December 2005.

~

In fact I didn't want to study journalism originally. It was all because famous universities in Beijing were miserly about giving good opportunities to graduating high school students from poor areas like mine, Guizhou Province. I wanted to study economics at Beijing University, but their economics department didn't recruit in our area. I took another look and the options left included journalism. Working as a journalist could be a showy job—you could just stick your microphone into someone's face and make him talk, quite powerful. I'd heard my aunt and uncle call reporters awesome! A Chinese saying describes reporters as always one class above the bureaucrats, which means that a reporter always ranks higher than the official he interviews. It seemed journalism could be a satisfactory profession and would be fun. So I enrolled in the journalism department of Renmin University.

When I got to college, I was confused to find I couldn't write well. I also started to stutter, and for awhile I couldn't speak either. I decided the fundamental reason for my bad writing was that I didn't know how to think. I wondered, how could this happen? I've lived nineteen years but still lack the ability to think. Freshman year was a relatively dangerous year at my university—some students found the world completely different from what they'd been taught, some failed to find themselves, some showed abnormal behavior, and some even killed themselves. My freshman year was very important to me; I was determined to learn to think. At that time, I also pondered life and death. When you think about issues, life and death are the fundamental ones. So I spent relatively a lot of time on thinking. And gradually I learned to speak again.

Then I began to think about why I really wanted to be a journalist. When freshman year was over, I thought I might have made the wrong choice. Our profession was supposed to speak out, but there were always people who wanted to criticize you and stop you. All that thinking at college went into my senior thesis. My topic was press freedom. The title was "Freedom of the Press: Fundamental Guarantee for the Smooth Functioning and Coordinated Development of Society." When I proposed this to my adviser, who also was the department chair, he said, "Don't you want to graduate?" I said those four characters—*xin wen zi you*, freedom of the press—have been on my mind throughout my four years in college. You can't forbid me to write about it.

My thesis said that, even if you're unwilling to talk about it, the concept of freedom of the press is very useful, a technique to make society safe, including the government itself. If you don't permit reporting and then everybody listens to Voice of America and the BBC, is that of any benefit to you? We are facing an open world and people have diverse channels for obtaining news, so you can't cover things up. If you try, you will reap just the opposite of what you wish. My teacher commended me for discussing freedom of the press from a sociological perspective, which was relatively rare. He gave it an A plus and I graduated in 1991. Then I went to work at Xinhua News Agency.

In all my time as a journalist since, there's been no moment I didn't think about those four words: freedom of the press.

My parents both were engineers, water supply and discharge experts, graduates of Chongqing Institute of Engineering. My father was from Guizhou and my mother from Sichuan. Upon graduation, they went to the poorest mountain area of Guizhou to build a new mine. It was a remote area where tigers still roamed—my father once asked me: Did you know a tiger left its footprints in front of our house? There was no kindergarten; my parents used to lock me inside when they went off to work. I would look at cartoon picture books and make drawings of the People's Liberation Army and Tiananmen Square.

During my early childhood, I had many good buddies from the surrounding countryside. When I started elementary school, however, I began to notice the differences. I could go to the best school, operated by the mine, but those peasant kids had to walk an hour or two to a dilapidated school. Those kids told me they had to climb over several mountains to reach their school. I could hardly imagine how they managed, since we were only about seven years old. I asked my father why they couldn't go to the same nearby school as me, and he said it was because they were from peasant families. I felt they were quite unfortunate. I started to wonder about these inequalities.

All around were huge mountains. It rained almost everyday, which got depressing. Say you wanted to go out and play—then the rain would come and ruin your plans. The mountains sat there all the time, which got me to wondering what was behind them—there must be sea or grassland or something I would like. One day when I was in ninth grade, I got a peasant buddy to climb a mountain with me. It took us awhile, and when we reached the top, all we saw were still more mountains! On the spot, I decided that by all means I had to go to school where Tiananmen Square was.

My father died when I was fourteen, just finishing middle school. One day he fell sick and the doctor said it was a common cold and didn't pay much attention. It turned out to be blood clots on the brain. He basically died of overwork. He'd worked all his life bringing water to the mine. One river passed by, but the water was undrinkable because of uranium pollution, so my father had to cross several mountains to find a clean water source. He found it eventually and designed a very good reservoir. He came from a peasant background and could handle hardship. He would work around the clock. Once in the middle of the winter, he dove several meters down to clear weeds out of a water filter. When peasants suffered drought and broke the water main for irrigation, which was illegal, he was able to calm them down. My father was a kind person. He'd studied Chinese herbal medicine on his own, and when peasants came to the mine to sell vegetables, they would drop in and my father would treat them with herbs.

I had four sisters—three older, one younger. After my father's death, my mother took care of the five of us, which wasn't easy. She told me not to study science, saying look what happened to your father—it will bring you much misery. She told me to pursue the humanities, saying those people could become officials and leaders and thus could be other people's bosses. My mother is a very down-to-earth person.

I attended college during the period when Chinese leaders were talking about increasing transparency. The school environment was quite open—you could go to symposiums and hear different voices, and everybody was expressing his own views on state affairs. Once I went to hear a professor from Taiwan give a talk. This guy thumped on the table and said he wanted to have a debate with Wang Zhen, vice president of the People's Republic of China! As a lad who'd just come out of the remote mountains, I thought, God, this is really something!

We journalism students paid a lot of attention to talk about drafting a press law. There were two views: Some thought the press should be open and free while others thought the press should be managed and censored. I worked on a weekly blackboard newspaper run by students themselves—it was just like a real newspaper in both writing style and layout. I had a press card bearing the seal of our Communist Youth League branch, which enabled me to interview anyone, so I would run around finding people I wanted to interview.

In the past, student journalists would interview the head of the campus mess hall, or the dormitory manager. Now when our reporting teacher sent us out to do interviews as homework, he was rattled at what we brought back—interviews with dissident physicist Fang Lizhi and people like that. I interviewed the Taiwanese writer Bo Yang, who visited Beijing in November 1988. I went to his hotel to see him. He said people should relate to one another as soul colliding with soul, but on this trip he perceived people locked in cages, so it was cages colliding with cages. He said Chinese people worshipped saints—Saint Confucius, Saint Chiang Kai-shek, Saint Mao, Saint Marx. He talked a lot; in fact, he talked for a whole morning. I wrote up the interview and handed it in.

I thought our blackboard paper was the greatest! No prior restraint. Every Saturday, we would put up the new issue at the school gate. It aroused great anxiety among the school leadership. The Party secretary would go take a look with a flashlight to see if there were any really bad things. On quite a few occasions he was furious. One time it was about Deng Xiaoping—who'd lit a cigarette during a meeting in the Great Hall of the People, prompting someone to pass him a note asking him to stop smoking in public, which he did. One of my schoolmates drew a cartoon showing Deng with a huge head and tiny body, puffing out a cloud of smoke with two characters inside—*gai ge*, reform. The school leaders were enraged and ordered it erased immediately. One advantage of our blackboard paper was that we could easily correct errors with a damp rag.

In those days, I was very mischievous and wrote a lot of stuff. Later I became chief editor of the blackboard paper. Our best issue was about the death of Hu Yaobang in the spring of 1989. It occupied two blackboards. *Science and Technology Daily* was the first to report on the crowds lining Chang'an Boulevard to watch the funeral motorcade, and I got an exclusive interview with the paper's deputy chief editor about how they got the news out. I also interviewed a member of the press law drafting committee about those issues. And we had an exclusive research report analyzing news coverage of earlier student demonstrations in 1986, arguing that the people wouldn't want to read *People's Daily* if it didn't report what was going on.

I thought this was the best I'd ever done. I wanted to continue—but our blackboards disappeared! Later on I saw them in Tiananmen Square; I took a look—hey, aren't these my blackboards? Someone was sleeping on them—he'd turned my blackboards into his bed. Very interesting. Afterwards, a classmate told me: Wang Jun, good thing somebody stole the blackboards, or you'd have been in big trouble. I answered: You are wrong; that theft halted a great newsman's work.

In April 1989, when students tried to shout down a speaker on campus whose views they disliked, I wrote a commentary titled "Advocates of Democracy, Please Do Not Hush up Others." I said the democratic attitude should be: While I fight to the death to oppose your viewpoint, I also fight to the death to defend your right to speak. To tell the truth, I wasn't very optimistic about the student movement, because I felt that few people of our generation knew much about democracy.

As for the demonstrations, I felt my role should be to observe and record. My adviser told me to stay out of trouble, and I said at this juncture I just wanted to find out exactly what was happening. *People's Daily* had reported that the standing committee of the National People's Congress would call an emergency meeting to discuss the issues involved. I thought that would be good, that we should follow procedures. But the students insisted on going on a hunger strike. Then the tragedy happened. I felt anguished. I felt I wouldn't see the democratization of China in my lifetime because our generation didn't understand democracy. They didn't know how to further their cause using tolerant methods. After June 4th, when I tried to pick up a book, I couldn't read a single word.

When classes resumed, I was supposed to resume the blackboard newspaper, but I wasn't in the mood. The department chair insisted I continue. So I wrote an editor's note, with several sentences that remain especially useful to me even today: "We must use our own eyes to observe, our own brains to think, our own hearts to feel, and our own hands to practice. We must follow such a path."

I went on to an internship at *China Youth Daily*. I started a column on the psychology of college students, which was a lot of fun. News from the college campuses then was very sensitive, so we reported things like: Why do college students skip classes? Why do they sit for graduate entrance exams? Why do they loathe weekends? We got help from students in the social sciences who needed to do studies for their homework—I asked for a survey on the rate of students skipping classes and whether it was going up or down over the semester, collaborations like that. What kept me going was my interest in the facts themselves. I felt we should use facts to solve problems instead of taking stands at the outset, which could end in tragedy. One of our professors put it very well: He said China had arrived at the quantitative age. In the past, our qualitative analysis was not based on quantitative analysis, so the latter could blow away the former. So at that time of distress, I suddenly found a reason to justify becoming a journalist. That is, to find out the truth about events, about humanity, and about society.

I decided there are three stages of being a journalist. The first is as an extraterrestrial being investigating the living conditions of the humans on the planet earth. The second is like a spectator in the front row of a theater, who can enjoy the show and see many details. The third is the little boy who points out that the emperor has no clothes. I want to be some of all three. All three are necessary.

After graduation I was assigned to Xinhua's Beijing bureau. I was hoping to continue reporting on education but instead got the urban construction beat. The leaders told me I'd be at a disadvantage because that beat didn't generate much news; unlike political and cultural reporting, where a single conference can generate a lot of dispatches, not many buildings and bridges are built in a year. The usual stories were things like Beijing is growing bigger, growing taller, growing prettier, et. I joined right in, writing things like Beijing ranks number one in the world for overpasses. Unmatched glory would be having our dispatches picked up by *People's Daily*. Looking back, it seems ridiculous.

Fortunately I gradually entered my role and did the stories that led to my book *Cheng Ji [Chronicle of a City]*, published in 2003. This book was the inevitable result of challenges I ran into in the course of my work. I have three

Beijing city officials to thank: the former mayor and two former vice mayors. I started running into conflicts with the city of Beijing beginning in 1995, and they put a lot of pressure on me. I say that, without pressure, chicks cannot hatch—thus my book was hatched.

The stuff I wrote for Xinhua wasn't that great. Even my longer pieces always contained things I was dissatisfied with. The book is different. Many friends who read it were puzzled: What kind of book is this? It has stories, it looks like literary reportage, but then again it doesn't because you didn't make it up and you didn't use techniques of fiction. You have lots of footnotes and document your sources, like in a scholarly work. Actually I oppose the Chinese tradition of *baogao wenxue*—literary reportage: If it is reporting, how can it be literature at the same time? I feel facts are facts, and facts can't be literary. Literature means fictionalization and exaggeration. Literature contains lots of adjectives. Journalists should use verbs, not adjectives. Neither do I accept writing methods that fail to provide sources of information, which is hugely questionable.

Journalism is connected to history. My book can be considered a lengthy report on our city today, addressing such questions as why life is so inconvenient now and how that's related to city planning decisions after 1949—how it's related to Chairman Mao's attitude at that time and to debates between the Soviets and Chinese scholars, especially preservationist Liang Sicheng, and the failure of his efforts that led to the wholesale dismantling of this ancient city, including the destruction of the city wall. There was even thought of tearing down the Forbidden City. Although these things happened decades ago, they still possess news value, because people didn't know about them and I dug them up.

Recently we had a college reunion, and my schoolmates said I could be counted as one of the lucky ones who maintain the typical college student mindset. In reporting and writing this book, I expressed and practiced the values I'd thought so much about in college.

I was the first to report on questionable procedures over the Oriental Plaza project, approved by the mayor himself, so he was furious with me. Thank God he later was removed from office; otherwise, I might be a petty merchant or cab driver now! My investigative reporting on losses from land deals in Beijing angered a vice mayor, who wanted to publish articles refuting me. My reporting about threats to historic preservation surrounding the former residence of Cai Yuanpei led to the conflicts with another vice mayor, who even accused me of sabotaging Beijing's bid to host the Olympics.

Back in 1995 when I began confronting these conflicts, I was a naïve lad. But from start to finish, I investigated from a journalist's standpoint. I didn't expect to run into so much trouble. If you asked me whether I was afraid then, I would say I was very afraid. I still didn't understand affairs thoroughly and wanted to find out the truth. Having finished my book, now I can declare that I am not afraid of them. If someday they murder me with a heavy brick, I will have died a worthy death. Had they killed me back then I would have been greatly wronged, for I wouldn't know what I'd died for.

Let me talk about the former residence of Cai Yuanpei—president of Beijing University during the May Fourth Movement, a great intellectual and educator whose status in China is like that of Voltaire in the European Enlightenment. In November 2000, a friend called to tell me Cai's house was being torn down. I said that was impossible, the house was a protected cultural heritage site, but he said he'd seen the character *chai*—to be demolished—on the wall and the dismantling had begun. I rushed there and was shocked to find my friend was right. If they dared to tear down Cai Yuanpei's house, it must be that all intellectuals in China were done for—I really had such a feeling. From the alley I could see the huge character on the wall and a smashed roof; and when I entered the courtyard I could see other roofs with gaping openings. Only one resident was still there. He showed me around. He was very distressed, not just because of the dismantling, but also because he couldn't understand how this could happen.

When I began to take photos and do interviews, the guy supervising the demolition rushed in fiercely to demand what I was up to. I told him I was from Xinhua News Agency. The guy said the house was too run down to be a cultural relic. I told him I knew he couldn't make decisions himself, but that he had to stop, and he could tell his superiors I was there. Then I returned to my office and wrote a report for our *neican*—the internally circulated reference news. Evidently officials got nervous when they found out about my visit, and they ordered the house repaired. Then, to show I was a liar and that nothing had happened, they invited other reporters to the site to take pictures, which were published in a couple of newspapers—taking up half a page in *Guangming Daily* and an entire page of *Beijing Youth News*.

The affair developed into a debate over whether Wang Jun and Xinhua were lying or not. We would have to fight for both my dignity and Xinhua's dignity. At this juncture, the Beijing municipal government called a press conference for a vice mayor to declare that Cai's former residence was under city protection and had never been dismantled. Afterwards, he came down from the podium to shake hands and make small talk with reporters. When he got to me, I identified myself as being from Xinhua, and he acted like a bull seeing a red cape. Let me tell you, he said, you must consider the consequences! Then he swaggered off.

When I got back to the office, I told my leaders that, although as vice mayor he had power and could threaten me, as a reporter I believed facts were bigger than power. I was prepared for this struggle: From the first day I'd witnessed the destruction of Cai's former residence, I'd visited the site daily and not just taken photos but also videotaped how they tore it apart and how they tried to repair it and how it looked after the repairs. I'd also sent the evidence over to my good buddies at the newspaper *Southern Weekend* and after the press conference urged them to use it; a week or so later they told me the pictures would run the next day. Meanwhile, the city was calling Xinhua asking me not to meddle in this matter or write about it anymore—claiming it was harming the bid for the Olympics. I said, first, the city of Beijing should answer squarely just who is lying? Second, they should answer squarely just who is sabotaging the Olympic bid—those who illegitimately destroy cultural relics or a reporter who exposes the phenomenon? Third, *Southern Weekend* is going to press and there is no time to stop it. Fourth, you can deal with me as severely as you like.

The next day the story was in *Southern Weekend*. It was stunningly good. On one side of the page were my pictures of the dismantling and repair and what it looked like after the repair, plus a short report I'd written; and on the other side were reports from various major newspapers claiming the destruction had never happened. An editor's note asked: Did these things that have drawn wide attention in Beijing ever happen or not? Different people have different opinions. I told my friends: This is so well done! You are very fair—both sides have their own opinions! Surely that vice mayor was grinding his teeth in murderous anger at me.

At that time, Beijing was bidding to host the Olympics, and was most concerned about its image. I'd written about how the development of China's urban economy depended on what I called *chaiqian*—literally, dismantling and removal, or condemnation and dislodging, to make way for real estate development.

In Beijing, for example, more than half of all social investment revolves around real estate, which relies on this process. If I tear down your house, you'll have to buy new housing. This demand from those in residential areas whose houses have been torn down for commercial construction makes up approximately one-third of the real estate market. For developers it is an especially good thing—they tear down housing, they get the land, they pay some compensation, and the displaced residents have to come back and buy new housing, but the money they got in compensation is not enough to buy new housing, so they'll go into debt. This accentuates the transfer of social wealth from the poor to the rich, and the gap between them grows.

I blew the whistle; I tried to expose these things and point out the harm such a development pattern would cause the country. I reasoned that the greatest problem China faces is the polarization of haves and have-nots. People who want to buy don't have the money while people who have the money don't need to buy, leading to China's huge dependence on foreign trade, which further weakens the domestic market. Our minister of commerce, Bo Xilai, has said that China exports 800 million shirts to buy one Airbus. This is really a dire situation. A few typhoons interrupting the oil supply could finish off the country; the situation is that fragile. And it all has to do with this demolition-relocation pattern in urban development.

The greatest challenge in journalism is self-censorship. When you write, you ask yourself if this and that are okay. During your first year, you think about it. By the second year, you begin to censor yourself. Even when no problem exists, you presume it does and kill it yourself. This is the most dreadful thing.

The worst period for me was in the mid-1990s. I just wrote things like overpasses growing bigger and buildings growing taller and so on and so forth. I didn't have my own style; no matter how I tried, it came out hackneyed. I decided that my mind was too fossilized and realized that I was subconsciously self-censoring. Even though I had good eyes, I wasn't seeing. I chastised myself: If I censor myself too much, I will lose my basic function as a reporter, which is to discover.

I didn't write anything that distorted facts, but I did write things that sounded like propaganda. But I tried to minimize those things. I joke that I can turn one fish into three dishes. For instance, in 2002 I wrote three articles about the central axis of Beijing. Two were ordinary Xinhua dispatches. The third was what I really wanted to write, about drastic changes and vicissitudes over the years, including the dismantling of three major city gates, and plans for the large Olympic arenas to be built on the north extension of the central axis. This ran in *Outlook Weekly*, a news magazine also published by Xinhua.

At year's end, I had to write how construction along the central axis reflected the correct policies of the Chinese Communist Party and slogans like the "three represents." I polished off that report in just over an hour. My colleagues liked my approach and asked if I could teach them to write this sort of major report so effortlessly. I suggested Xinhua invent a computer software program so that whenever a reporter typed a leader's name, the phrase "great, glorious, and correct" would pop out; and whenever one typed something frowned upon like *falungong*, the banned spiritual cult, the computer would quietly prompt for criticism. This way no mistakes would ever be made.

After I'd wised up, the Beijing branch wanted me to write about how great Chang'an Boulevard was, but I resolutely refused; I absolutely could not write that, because Chang'an Boulevard was a complete failure. Looking back—how should I put it?—I did a lot of things against my will. At times my wife would say I might as well quit a job that sometimes seemed both meaningless and tiring. But as I later told a younger reporter, this is an imperfect world, so one must pay a price to live in it. However, when I pay the price, I need to know specifically what I want and must have.

In 2004 I transferred to *Outlook Weekly*, where I'm deputy director of the culture department and have more latitude. There are many things people say we can't report—and yet, we report them. I also am working on three more books and have ideas for others. I could make a living from writing books. Humanity needs ideals—but ideals are marketable. I can write a book that contains ideals, and people with ideals will spend money on it.

The past twenty years have brought obvious changes in China's journalism. In the past, many celebrated journalists did not consider journalism their profession; rather, they were fiction writers who also wrote literary reportage that read like novels. In this mode, the writer takes a stand from the very beginning. When he says a man is bad, the man is bad to an extreme and can never change for the good. In reality, human nature is very complex. In the late 1980s, a novelistic scholarly style emerged, with scientific and Western ideas tucked in, but still literary reportage. In the 1990s, as market-driven media evolved, journalists with truly professional attitudes began to emerge. They do things according to journalistic criteria. They don't hawk ads.

I myself am a product of this process. It used to be that writing a news report was like writing a court verdict: At the very outset, I said this guy is condemned, and then I demonstrated the evidence for his crimes. How can this be called reporting? Now, however, journalists are writing genuine news, paying attention to telling details, facts, and sources, and developing standards for reporting and writing. These changes are excellent.

A change for the worse is that everybody is too pressed for time. Media bosses are like capitalists: I give you this topic and you must get it done next week, and if you can't I'll withhold part of your salary. Market-directed journalists are under a lot of stress. They don't have any room for bargaining. They are forced to overwork until they drop. Gathering and putting out news in this fashion is counter to journalistic principles, so the quality is bound to be low. High quality requires many intermediate steps and can't be compressed; news can't be produced like widgets within a prescribed time limit.

Now many journalists complain that market-oriented media care too much about money, are too submissive to market forces and capital, work journalists too hard, etc. To the contrary, I think the transformation of Chinese media into enterprises relying on the market constitutes progress. I think the shortcomings are due to insufficient competition. Truly competitive media would operate according to journalistic standards and rely on high quality to win out in the marketplace.

Journalism and propaganda are two different things; propaganda uses facts as its means while journalism takes facts as its ends. I believe the ultimate goal of journalism is to find facts. Make facts the ends, not the means. In the past, too many people have sought facts as a means to achieve certain ends, while very few considered facts as the ends of the pursuit. Eventually we should take life as the ends, not the means. In the past, people haven't put life at the supreme level. In my work over the past decade and more, I have tried to do my job exactly this way.

I think the greatest gift a reporter can have is curiosity. If you're especially curious about something, you want to make discoveries about it. I feel greatly satisfied when I learn the facts. Once all the reporters were going after one official about a very sensitive question, and he chose me to be the only reporter to talk to. In a hotel room he shut the door and said more than a hundred journalists, domestic and foreign, want to talk to me, but I'm refusing them all. I want to talk to you about the facts of this matter. Why? Because I'm familiar with your work and I trust you. So he talked to me for a whole night. When I was done and walked out onto the street, I felt I was a real reporter. This made me joyful.

Architects talk about their three Hs: Some people draw with their hands, some with their heads, and some with their hearts. Of course, the best is to draw with the heart. However, hands are also important, so you can draw whatever clients want and finish it and sign the contracts. What I do at Xinhua is but a job; if I can write what my boss wants and hand it over, it's okay. I deal with him with my hands, not my heart. When I write for internal reference publications, then I use my head. I keep my heart for myself—my book and other research projects, they belong to me. I don't pound on the table at Xinhua and demand they publish my stuff. I do my own things.

Since 1995 I've been writing up my interview notes, everything I consider relatively important experiences. Sometimes I review what I wrote ten years ago and feel moved by the fact that I inscribed all these details of history. I can write 100,000 to 200,000 characters in a sitting at my home computer, and feel comfortable and happy because there is no censorship. I sing my own tune, and sing it freely. I don't self-censor. Nor do I seek to get this published.

Over time, I've come to feel that writing is my existential state. When I first heard about the mountaineer who said he climbed mountains because the mountains were there, I thought that was stupid. Now I understand. For the same reason, a reporter must report because the facts are there. The greatest reward of my work is learning about the facts, knowing the truth. I've cultivated the stance that publishing doesn't really matter to me. I think my best writing is my reporting notes. Of course my book is also very good. I didn't write it for publication, so it contained my own words. Actually I was surprised that it got published. And nothing bad happened to me afterwards.

Over the past couple of years, my interest in the values underlying freedom of the press has grown even stronger. In this era, we must rely on a free media to play a more active role. I hope the whole society and especially the authorities will come to identify with the values of freedom of the press.

The purpose of our work is to communicate, not just to disseminate. When a society can communicate, then it can function well. Communication can lead to consensus and construction in its real sense, and love among people. Otherwise there will be hatred and misunderstanding. Looking back over Chinese history, what was lacking for several thousand years was good communication, without which some people groundlessly tended to see other people as monsters and they thus inexorably become monsters. Our work is to change this situation. I feel this profession indeed is worth devoting my life to.

• 2 •

Zhou Yijun
周轶君

Then: Xinhua News Agency
新华社
Now: Phoenix TV, Hong Kong
凤凰电视

*M*ultilingual, adept at multimedia, always looking to learn, Zhou Yijun gets places few young Chinese women go. Fluent in Arabic and English, she spent two years in Gaza as a correspondent for Xinhua News Agency, earning recognition for writings and pictures that captured emotion along with news. She was an early blogger and is an accomplished photographer. When we spoke with her in December 2005, she was back at Xinhua's Arabic division in Beijing and tiring of office-bound translation work. In late 2006, at age thirty, she left what could have been a lifelong sinecure for a job at Phoenix TV's main newsroom in Hong Kong. Phoenix, a private enterprise begun in 2000 by a former Chinese army officer, broadcasts over satellite in Mandarin, with programming that gently presses the bounds of convention without alienating mainland authorities. Zhou found the transition rough: "My boss was not happy with my hairstyle, makeup, or speed of speaking," she e-mailed. And she felt a bit lonely in Hong Kong. But she also felt her expertise was being used. She's called on to explain news from the Middle East, and has returned to the region on reporting trips. And on top of Shanghai dialect, Mandarin, and her two foreign languages, she was learning Cantonese.

I grew up in Shanghai and came to Beijing for higher education at eighteen. My father had wanted to become a journalist, but his job had nothing to do with journalism; he worked in an auto repair factory. My mother was an accountant in a machinery factory. When I was little, my parents had an old-fashioned camera and I became very interested in photography. I learned some basics at a neighborhood children's center, not a lot, but later on I found that, when you grow up, you might come to reconnect with childhood interests.

I attended the Second Foreign Languages Institute in Beijing. My college major was Arabic language and literature. Most of us majoring in foreign languages thought we didn't have a real major, that we'd have to study other fields to get by in the real world. I made my mind up to become a foreign correspondent when I was a sophomore. It seems to have been a natural path, my destiny. I looked up to people like Tang Shizeng, one of the earliest Chinese reporters sent over to the Middle East to report on the first Gulf War.

I've had little systematic education in journalism. More often than not, I've explored through practice. I didn't take journalism courses in college, but from sophomore year to graduation I did help run a student newspaper, even becoming head of the reporting group. I still have those issues of *College Life* we produced. When I reread the stories I wrote, they sound infantile. Even so, I gradually made discoveries and improved, and felt that my dream of becoming a real journalist was drawing closer each day.

My senior year, I decided to seek a job with Xinhua's *guojibu*, the international news department. I brought over my resume and was told that, even if I scored number one on the qualification exam, they still wouldn't hire me—the reason being that I'm female. They said they wanted only males, especially for reporting from Arabic countries. Girls would cause more trouble—pregnancy, childbirth, etc. I tried twice, but was definitely turned down. At the time, I thought that eventually I would prove them wrong and get this job. Some of my male competitors might have been very capable, but nobody had a passion stronger than mine.

Meanwhile, I took the exam for Xinhua's *duiwaibu*, the external news department—which puts out dispatches in other languages for foreign readers—and was hired in the Arabic section. I began my career at Xinhua in 1998. The early days were disappointing. I spent my time translating articles, most quite boring. There seemed little relationship between what I was doing day in and day out and the kind of challenging work I'd dreamed of doing.

I decided that I had to find some fun in my work, and started going out on my own to find news. Because our department's job was to report on China for foreign readers, I went looking for stories on *Niu Jie*—Ox Street, a Muslim residential area in Beijing. At last I felt I was gathering news myself, and my work suddenly began to make sense.

I could have used some guidance, but got none. The exception was a three-month training course in 1999, run jointly by Xinhua and the Thompson Foundation of Britain. Those three months were very fruitful. I wrote stories in English every day, and two teachers corrected them. They always encouraged me; although my written English wasn't the best in the class, they would commend my mastery of grammar. They were good at discovering your strong points; if they thought you were a good photographer, they'd assign you a photo job; or they would praise you for the detail in your story and use it as a model for the whole class to discuss. This sort of care, help, and mentorship motivated us.

In 2002, I heard that Xinhua had a spot open in Gaza and decided to apply. I wrote two letters requesting the job, and was turned down. A supervisor explained to me that people worried about me as a girl even in Beijing, so how could they feel at ease if I went that far away?

One night soon after, I served as Arabic interpreter for a deputy director of Xinhua who was hosting a banquet for visitors from Egypt. The next day I handed him a letter, telling him of my desire to go work in Gaza. He forwarded the letter to the personnel bureau.

The personnel director came to talk to me. He said: I have no concerns about your qualifications for this job, but you know what I am worried about? I said: You worry whether I can last there, right? Then I told him: A male colleague may be superior in muscle power, but as a female I may have better endurance. I would be going to Gaza not for two weeks, but for two years. Under such circumstances, endurance would enable me to persevere.

I had expected the personnel director to tell me to give it up and that my supervisors were only thinking of my best interests. To my surprise, he said, "Gal, I like you. You can go with my blessing." After talking with me for only ten minutes or so, he'd agreed! It was beyond my wildest expectations.

An incident my very first week in the Mideast taught me how unprepared I was. Before going overseas, I'd taken driving lessons, since a reporter needed that skill. I got my driver's license in a month, but there was much about driving I still didn't know. I'd just gotten to Jerusalem when my car broke down. I called my colleague at the Xinhua bureau, who said my battery must be dead and that I could stop a car to get a jump start. I happened to wave down a CNN car. One of the passengers was a famous Palestinian reporter I knew. He asked me what was wrong and I told him. He asked if I had jumper cables, and I said no. What about water? No. First aid supplies? No. I felt really ashamed of myself.

Later I acquired all these things, and would even go out of my way to help jump-start Palestinians' cars. I realized I had the necessary courage but lacked practical experience. Other than a pamphlet I'd picked up during the

Thompson Foundation course, called "Journalists in a War Zone," I'd had no preparation in this regard. After returning from the Mideast, I gave this pamphlet to China's Foreign Ministry, which planned to have it translated into Chinese for reporters going overseas in the future.

My office in Gaza was on the Palestinian side. A local friend told me that one of his employees lived near a relatively large Jewish settlement and always came to work sleepy; every night was like war near his home, with almost continuous gunfire. To the Palestinians, the settlements are terrifying places. They cannot get close; nor do they know what life inside is like. I decided to see for myself what it was really like both inside and outside the settlements.

On the plane going over, I'd sat next to an Israeli whose children lived in a settlement and had taken his phone number on the spot, thinking it might come in handy one day. I got in touch with him about my story and he agreed to help.

I told the Palestinian who lived by the settlement that I'd like to stay overnight at his home and see what life was like, and he was delighted, since few foreigners went there. When I arrived in my Jeep, several hundred excited children lined the streets to greet me.

From my host's home, one could see a settlement in the distance, but Palestinians were not allowed within seven to eight hundred meters. That evening, as we cooled off and chatted in the courtyard, gunshots suddenly sounded, so we hurriedly collected the cushions and ran inside. A child said his shoes were still in the yard, but his mother told him to leave them there. The gunshots served as a warning not to go out because at 7 p.m. curfew would be enforced. Everyone was panic stricken. They said that, although this was a daily occurrence, they still felt scared when it happened. They told me about a Palestinian worker who'd been out past curfew recently; the electric drill he was holding was mistaken for a gun, and he was killed on the spot. People outside after 7 p.m. would sing as they walked to signal the Israelis that they had no weapons with them.

That night I shared the panic. My hosts insisted that, as their guest, I sleep in a bed while they slept on the floor. We stayed awake past midnight. From time to time, we'd hear more gunshots, explosions, and tanks on patrol rumbling right outside the windows. The family told me their most frightening experience had been when the Israelis fired the tanks' big guns. They'd taken cover in the bathroom, the spot in the house furthest from the settlements—although the whole house measured only forty or fifty square meters, so it didn't make much difference where you hid. The next morning they found the tracks left by the tank treads and several holes in their sheep pen from the shelling.

A few days later, I visited a settlement. It was a complete change of scene: beautiful, with well-spaced cottages, flowers blooming, birds chirping, and so on. You still could hear tanks firing, but it was just soldiers drilling. The Israelis didn't seem as hospitable as the Palestinians, nor did I ask to spend the night, so I stayed the day and left at sunset. The residents had moved there from the Sinai Peninsula in the 1970s, when the Israeli government planned to pull down their original settlement. They were afraid government policy might change again and they might have to move again. So the Jews felt they were victims as well, and weren't happy either.

The result was a story titled "Inside and Outside the Settlements," contrasting the two places and the feelings of their residents. I'd always thought the Palestinians were more terrified of the Jews with their guns and tanks than the other way around. But a Palestinian told me: No, we are the scary ones and they are afraid of us. There are more of us. Why do they fire guns? They shoot because they are scared. Their settlements are like isolated islands in the middle of the Palestinian sea. So their side is more scared.

On February 7, 2004, around 9 on another ordinary morning, I heard a loud bang outside and knew immediately there must have been another explosion somewhere in Gaza. I turned on the radio, which was reporting that a missile had hit a car and wounded three people, including a leader of the radical Palestinian group Jihad. If I went to the spot, all I'd get would be the same old sort of pictures, showing totally destroyed cars. Then the radio said a small boy had suffered serious injuries. I decided to go to the hospital to see how this child was doing. As I was driving there, the radio was still reporting that the little boy was seriously wounded and that doctors were trying to save him. So I rushed to the emergency room—Palestinian hospitals are not very modernized, so anyone can walk in. The little boy was lying on a bed, and several doctors were putting tubes in him. I started taking pictures. As I was snapping away, through the viewfinder I saw a doctor pull a white sheet over the boy. Then that doctor saw me and angrily shoved me toward the door, telling me to stop taking pictures. I was so engrossed that I didn't respond; only after getting pushed outside the room did I realize the little boy had just died. He'd died while I was photographing him.

I felt especially sad. I'd been in Gaza for a year and a half and had seen death up close many times. However, this was the first time a life had actually vanished right in front of my lens. That day I did something I think was very unprofessional for a journalist. Usually I'd go back to my office to send dispatches, write features, and so on. This time I phoned my editor in Beijing and told him I had something to do and couldn't return to my office, but I could file an oral report. I gave him a rough version of the story. Then I went to the little boy's home to attend his funeral, and to the graveyard for his burial. I felt that only after seeing him be buried could my heart begin to settle down.

By now, all the photojournalists were gone—they'd taken pictures of the destroyed car and of people shooting into the air and shouting slogans at the funeral, gotten whatever they needed and stopped work for the day. But I had a strong desire to follow the funeral procession to the graveyard and watch the child be laid to rest. It took more than three hours and my pictures went out late.

The next day and the day after, I went to the boy's home to see his parents. On my last visit, his mother sat there woodenly, without tears. That boy was the family's only son. A relative who saw me photographing brought a picture of the boy, a martyr's picture, and put it behind the mother as background. When the mother saw the picture, she suddenly burst into tears. I couldn't go on. I told them I couldn't take pictures any more and had to leave.

Another person seriously wounded in that incident was a Palestinian, aged fifty-one, who supported a family of thirteen people. Now he was unable to work, and they had to rely on United Nations relief rations. I visited their house, which didn't even have a door or glass in the window. There was no electricity. Water came from a well. Without money, the daughter could only attend a free religious school run by Hamas.

I wrote a story about these experiences titled "After an Ordinary Bombing." The world wouldn't pay much attention to it. But for those victims, it took away everything.

Xinhua offers opportunities to report on different areas, and many topics pertain to more than one area. I feel my biggest challenge is lack of knowledge: I always know too little and need to do a lot of homework. In 2001, I was part of the team covering the Ninth National Games in Guangzhou. I wasn't that interested in sports to start with, so I knew even less about it than other things. But I figured that, since I was there, I had to find material and do my job well. And actually my perspective as a nonexpert allowed me to find interesting things that didn't necessarily require specialized knowledge. For example, I saw a girl of seven or eight practicing gymnastics who had scars on her wrists. We chatted, and she told me about the hardships of training. It occurred to me that, while only a small number of people will win medals in this field, so many little girls like this one were training quietly with big dreams, which might be the most beautiful aspect of sports. I wrote a story about it that people liked a lot.

The worst part of my job is sitting in the office. Now that I'm back in Beijing, I sit in the office every day and write news based on secondhand materials. This makes for a feeling of distance—to use Chinese sayings, you are "watching the fire from across the river" or "scratching an itch from outside your boots." But even under such circumstances, there are always things worth learning. For instance, although I reported firsthand on Palestine and Israel, I wasn't well informed about other Mideast issues, such as Syria and Lebanon. In my current work, I have to cover all the major events and hottest issues of the region. This forces me to read a lot; only then can I write features and analytical articles. Gradually I've learned not to complain, but rather to learn more from the process.

If I were reporting on domestic news, I think the biggest reward would be to do stories that would lead to change. Since I do international news, changes in this regard are rare. The biggest joy of my work is getting to witness many things. I want to tell stories in a different way from others—perhaps with more detail, and from a woman's standpoint. After reading my story on the settlements, one colleague told me he'd never read such vivid reporting before. He may have been talking casually, but the words are burned into my memory. I felt I was getting major recognition.

I used to think the most important thing for a reporter was to be where the news is and be the first to know. Now I feel a reporter should be able to effect change. Your reporting should move people and motivate people to change the world. Maybe this is too idealistic.

Young people who want to be journalists must, first, study and, second, recognize that they should never be the heroes of the story. It's fashionable for journalists to become stars, and many just follow fads. Perhaps they don't have much news to report. A journalist must be curious, and must be humble. Your subjects must always feel respected; only then can you find more things out. Journalism must tell the truth. China has a special environment—but more and more, in international news, I feel there's nothing I cannot talk about. The key is how you say it. China cares very much about keeping a certain balance, so on many issues we can't just follow Western media. We must have our own ideas and report issues from many sides.

Journalism progresses along with the larger environment. As our country grows more and more self-confident, journalism is bound to become more and more open. But we have to admit that we still have many problems. I think our country has made relatively rapid adjustments to new technologies. Blogs are a major development; now almost anybody can write a blog and say anything he likes. Of course, those that endanger the state are not allowed—but perhaps the same is true for every country.

As a journalist, I abhor predictions. If I had to predict for myself, I would say I can learn a lot of things in the next five or ten years and become more professional in my trade. I hope a good newspaper for international news in its true sense will emerge in China—there are such papers, but too few, and for various reasons, several have been closed down. The best known now is *Global Times*. To tell the truth, those of us who work in this field don't like it much because it tends to use sensational items to cater to readers and its content is not always true. But the masses like to read such stuff. It's important to find equilibrium among truthfulness, professionalism, and readability.

Before I got home from Gaza, I was getting attention from Chinese media—because they learned I was a woman. Now leaders of the international department sometimes tell others who are going abroad to go have a chat with Zhou Yijun. Indeed, I like sharing my thoughts; other people can learn from my experiences. I also write a blog. Many journalists have blogs. Recently I gave a series of lectures at my alma mater, and found out that many kids wanted to become war reporters. A lot of them want to be Robert Capa. I told them: You all want to be Capa, but what makes him memorable are his photographs, not the fact that he stepped on a landmine. He didn't want to die. You must know that, for war reporters, not a single story is worth your life. I hope to influence a few people; this would make me happy.

Lin Gu
林 谷

Then: China Features
中 国 特 稿 社
Now: Television editor and
journalism teacher

$\mathcal{L}$in Gu's mother, a former journalist, was uneasy at the idea of him working in the same field, thinking he might be too bold and outspoken for his own good. Lin Gu himself anticipated that working in Beijing, the center of Chinese politics, might be especially confining. He contends that has not been the case—to the contrary, he sees it as the eye of the storm and his preferred base. When we conversed in late 2005, he was still at China Features, an office of Xinhua News Agency that produces in-depth stories in English, often on contract for international publications. He has a master's in social anthropology from the University of Cambridge, England, and near-native command of English, which led the BBC to invite him to record a series of "letters from China." In 2006, the Graduate School of Journalism at the University of California-Berkeley invited him to spend an academic year in residence as a visiting scholar, and he resigned from Xinhua to accept the offer. He returned to Beijing in the spring of 2007 and e-mailed that he was mulling over options and considering becoming "a full-fledged freelance reporter in order to single-heartedly work on things I really feel passionate about." Within a few months, however, he had a job as an editor on a new weekly talk show on China Central Television, and was also teaching college journalism.

~

I am from Sichuan Province, whose spicy food is the most famous under the sun!

Basically, I became a journalist by accident. I was a philosophy major at Chengdu Institute of Technology, and did a master's in comparative literature at Shanghai International Studies University. After finishing graduate school, in June 1998, I expected to stay on as a language and literature teacher.

It so happened that Xinhua News Agency sent a fairly large recruiting group to our campus. My former roommate was working for Xinhua, so I asked one of the Xinhua people how he was doing. The man said he was doing fine and asked if I would like to apply.

I said first I would challenge him with a question: Do we have freedom of press and freedom of speech? And if the answer is negative, then why would one want to be a journalist? His response was not at all bureaucratic. He said the answer in a sense was negative, but that as a journalist you still could expand your own space, and that China's largest news organizations such as Xinhua allow space for you to put your abilities to good use.

My second question was whether I had to be a Communist Party member to work at Xinhua. He said you didn't have to be, that he himself wasn't. So it seemed to be a place I could contemplate going.

There also was a family factor—my mother had been a first-generation broadcaster for a radio station in the 1950s and worked as a journalist later on. My father was a college professor, so that occupation was an option, too.

Still, I was inclined to pursue a relatively simple life in the ivory tower of the university, so I didn't register for Xinhua's written test. To my surprise, the Xinhua man came to my dorm room and proposed that I take the test anyway, saying that, if I passed, I could always decline, and then boast about turning Xinhua down. I took the test, passed, and went to interview in Beijing at their expense.

Ten or so people sat across from me to ask questions. They asked my views on the idea that the foreign news media "demonize" China. I didn't realize that the main author of the book *Behind the Demonization of China*, Li Xiguang, was among the interviewers. I said I thought the book was somewhat biased, and that perhaps Chinese journalists also had problems of prejudice and stereotyped thinking when reporting on foreign countries, so we shouldn't blame foreign journalists alone for a problem both Chinese and foreign journalists should try to overcome. One interviewer cast a meaningful look at Li Xiguang and everybody smiled. I got through and was invited to work at Xinhua.

My understanding then was that being a good journalist required excellent interpersonal communication skills. You needed to make people feel comfortable, and just being friendly wasn't enough; you had to be sincere, and then people would open their hearts to you. Sincerity—this is the calling card of a good interviewer. The greatest luxury of this profession is that door after door opens to you, and you can then step into new worlds.

I discovered that I especially liked interviewing—people would spend most of the day telling you their life stories and confiding their innermost feelings. But when I went to write, I would agonize over how to begin. Once you return to the office and sit down to face the blank screen, you have to deliver something.

I started out doing hard news, and easily picked up the formulas, but quickly tired of Xinhua style. Many young journalists with innovative ideas run into old-fashioned editors who turn their stories into the same old Xinhua formats. Such editors are sometimes called "professional killers"—their news sense is reversed, so they can immediately find the elements with news value and cut them out! These editors themselves were once passionate and full of ideas, but over time they may have internalized this editing mentality.

Young journalists need mentors. A good editor is like a spouse; if you don't find the right person, it will be hard just to get a divorce. When I first got to Xinhua, I was assigned to an editor whose type didn't suit me, so I found another on my own and told him I'd follow him for a month. Together, for a project about China's reforms over the previous twenty years, we interviewed several chief editors at major newspapers about changes in the Chinese media. Xinhua had a rule that newcomers must stay in the office for three months editing copy, but I was disobedient—I didn't give a damn about the rules, and ran all around. Interestingly enough, nobody discouraged me or told me to stay in my office instead of running amok. I showed I could deliver. Young people should run around, and only later sit in the newsroom to do editing. I think it's ridiculous for young reporters to start as editors.

I was lucky to move on to China Features, which has relative editorial independence. It's not like the hard news department, where sometimes you feel so disgusted at the edited version of your story that you don't want your byline on it. Actually, there's no reason for Xinhua to adhere to the old mode.

I try to educate my Western colleagues not to think of Xinhua as a monolithic entity. It's multifaceted. To be sure, Xinhua is China's official national news agency. It has incomparable advantages over other media, such as superior access to information. It's making efforts to adapt to market changes by launching more market-oriented magazines, and its website is becoming a powerful player on the Internet. But beyond that, Xinhua has a lot of talented people. Xinhua journalists may write Xinhua-style stuff for the newspapers, but their features and in-depth reports are rich in news and detail.

One of my editors once said: The moment the central propaganda department tells us not to report something is the moment I begin to pay attention to it! I think that summarizes our way of working at China Features. We are problem-oriented. We tackle all sorts of issues, from suicide among rural women to domestic violence, homosexuality, gender inequality, and the AIDS crisis. We don't just say our great motherland is flourishing and strong; we seriously observe and think and address problems and look for solutions. Hong Kong's *South China Morning Post* feels at ease with us and uses many of our stories.

In China Features, I often come up with my own story ideas—for instance, somebody from the Chinese Academy of Social Sciences told me about Zhou Litai, a labor rights lawyer in Shenzhen who represents migrant workers. It sounded like a fascinating story, and I decided I had to go to Shenzhen to interview him. Of course I discuss ideas with my editor and get the go-ahead—otherwise my expenses won't be reimbursed.

Many of Zhou's clients were teenagers from the countryside. They'd come to the city thinking the streets were paved with gold, only to have their dreams shattered by the harsh realities of the sweatshop. Some of these youngsters lost limbs due to antiquated machinery or work pressure, and they'd get kicked out of the factories and couldn't even find a place to stay, let alone legal guidance. Zhou had assembled a kind of makeshift family, renting a three-story building in the Shenzhen outskirts to accommodate twenty to thirty clients, and living there also. I lived with them for a week.

Zhou himself had been a migrant worker and didn't forget where he came from; as a lawyer he was devoted to serving marginalized people. Many of the workers were from my home province of Sichuan, or from Chongqing municipality, which used to be part of Sichuan, and we spoke similar dialects. I felt I was seeing a corner of primitive capitalism in what we call a socialist country. The contrast was shocking.

I listened to the laborers' stories, and interviewed officials at the local court about how they handle these labor disputes, including a judge who was willing to share her views. Back in Beijing, I interviewed an official at the Ministry of Labor, who was quite candid, as well as a labor expert from Renmin University, who had frank comments on the dismal labor conditions in China.

Even though the topic was sensitive, my story did not get censored, and we sent it to the *South China Morning Post*, which gave it an entire page. Readers reacted strongly. Some brought Zhou Litai donations. A number of international news organizations, including *Time* and *Newsweek* and the BBC, subsequently interviewed him. Zhou became an international celebrity. I felt gratified that my reporting had some impact.

Covering this story enabled me to see beyond Shenzhen's skyscrapers. In Zhou Litai's makeshift family, different stories unfolded. A young laborer, only seventeen or eighteen, wondered what he could do without his right arm. He told me he wanted to study law and help people like lawyer Zhou had done. At that time, I thought he was just talking, but actually he was already taking law courses and preparing for licensing exams. Later I learned that he'd organized a small NGO to carry out labor law education among migrant laborers in Shenzhen. Some of the others returned to their home villages and resumed farming, leading quiet lives with the money Zhou had helped them win.

For another story, I went to Guangxi Province, on the Sino-Vietnamese border, to cover the AIDS crisis. I spent an afternoon at a rehab center for drug addicts. When you land there like a paratrooper, why should people open their hearts to you? I didn't expect them to. Usually local officials insist on escorting you. To my surprise, the young director of the center was very cooperative and said I could talk to the patients on my own for as long as I wished. This story also got a whole page in the *South China Morning Post*. I wrote a version in Chinese that we sent to *Southern Weekend*. At first, there was a long silence, so we figured they didn't want it. Suddenly there it was on the investigative reports page, under a joint byline—they'd done some double-checking and sent their own reporter, who added details.

Another story I wrote for *Southern Weekend* concerned a hospital in Beijing that was testing drugs on AIDS patients without informed consent. Peasants who had been infected with HIV from selling blood thought they were getting free treatment. Some died. *Southern Weekend* used this as a cover story, along with our commentary about informed consent as a human right. The hospital was very upset.

When you report on activists who are trying their best to help marginalized, vulnerable people, sometimes you really want to roll up your own sleeves and join them in the fight—become a story maker rather than just a storyteller.

The word *xuanchuan*—propaganda, although the Chinese now translate it as "publicity" —conveys hard sell, dictating, one-sided wishful thinking. I have deep antipathy toward propaganda. I think, after the founding of the People's Republic of China, the assumption was that our great achievements must be publicized. As a matter of fact, there were many great and beautiful things, but the salesmen spoiled it—they had fine goods, but they hawked them wrong, turning them into unmarketable goods.

Propaganda departments should serve reporters instead of trying to control them. Propaganda departments at all levels should be information departments—beyond just changing their English name to publicity, they've got to provide something. They must cooperate with reporters' newsgathering, take initiative to give reporters leads, and learn to think the way reporters think. Otherwise they'll just be a stumbling block for reporters.

Actually, propaganda departments everywhere obstruct reporters from their work, whether it's covering the White House or dealing with the military as a war correspondent. Universally, one of our missions is to challenge officialdom.

China still imposes many restrictions on journalists, especially in the provinces. Journalists in the provinces are controlled by local and provincial propaganda departments, not to mention the central propaganda department. And news control in a city like Shanghai is very strict; its elaborate development ambitions make for a paranoid propaganda department.

I think the best place to be a journalist is Beijing—here in the political center, "at the feet of the son of heaven," as we say. Beijing journalists in fact have much more leeway and room to maneuver. We don't have to take absolute orders from anyone, even though the central propaganda department is still there.

The greatest external challenge is from sources not wanting you to report. Government officials or other individuals, to protect themselves or their departmental interests, keep silent, lie, or request that you withhold facts. These are challenges from the system, but there are also professional challenges. Sometimes the reporter has to consider tradeoffs or compromises because a story might affect a person's reputation or his life. Sometimes you can't tell everything because of privacy considerations or other practical concerns. Handling this requires understanding and listening to and sometimes sympathizing with your interviewees. Reporters who violate confidentiality go against fundamental professional ethics.

There's yet another challenge. We complain a lot about censorship, but sometimes the fault lies with the reporter for not doing his homework. News control exists everywhere, be it on a battlefield in Iraq or on a quiet street in a small town in China. The question is how to be professional, how to be fair to your interviewees, how to make balanced reports, how to convey different voices and different sides. All these areas could be improved. You have to be quick and open-minded. You can't be afraid to ask tough questions—your only concern is that your interviewee may be offended and refuse to speak to you anymore.

Some reporters are lazy; rather than dig up their own stories, they wait for others to deliver. They show up at press conferences, slightly edit the press releases, and then claim them as their own reports. The issue of paid news, or so-called *hongbao*, "red envelopes," is worth mentioning. Journalists, especially those covering business, have lots of opportunities to attend press conferences and collect envelopes of "transportation fees" ranging from 200 to 500 yuan, or even more. I know people working for big companies or public relations firms whose job is to seduce journalists this way. Some reporters run from press conference to press conference just to collect cash. I call this bribery journalism; it's rampant, and it's a serious problem. If you take money, automatically you've lost your balance. Of course, this happens because there's a market for it. Ultimately journalists need to be paid more to guard against corruption.

The gratifications of this work are many. A reporter gets to travel at others' expense. How marvelous! Free travel, and at the end of the day you write something and get paid for it—a real bargain. Of course, as a journalist, you can't fully appreciate the scenery. You've got to focus on, gosh, the clock is ticking, and I haven't even found my contact! But basically it is pretty cool.

Another reward is that individuals you interview may become lifelong friends—such as lawyer Zhou. Perhaps in the midst of reporting, you want to remain impartial and objective, even keeping a distance; but once your interview is over—since a journalist is a human being, not an interviewing machine—you feel this person is worth befriending. At this moment, you go back to being an ordinary person. Journalism is a convenient way to make authentic friends.

One of the greatest changes in Chinese society is the heightened consciousness of rights. The Chinese Constitution was modified to include respect for human rights and the inviolability of private property. When large-scale demolition was taking place in Beijing, the media gave attention to an old man standing in front of a bulldozer holding a copy of the Constitution and proclaiming the defense of his home. This highly symbolic act showed that an ordinary person, an insignificant man, could pick up the Constitution to safeguard his rights. As the lunar new year approaches, media give headlines to marginalized groups like migrant workers who are owed pay by employers.

More professional news organizations have emerged. Professional journalists use fewer adjectives and more verbs and describe trends in a calm and objective manner. This is different from the heyday of literary reportage in the 1980s, which characterized things as either black or white, bad guys rotten to the core versus good guys praised to the skies. There is more serious investigative reporting and an emergence of standards.

The increased consciousness of rights also presents a challenge to journalism, since it involves clashes among different stakeholders. As a reporter, will you take sides? How far can you go? How to maintain your impartiality? Generally speaking, government voices are dominant in our mainstream media, whereas popular voices are relatively weak. Some reporters argue for giving the populace more space and time in a given story, in order to reach a relative balance overall. Others believe that, within a single story, you should seek balance.

It's easy to sympathize with the weak. Sometimes the facts make it clear that bureaucrats have ridden roughshod over ordinary people. Still, I think you should try to be fair even if you can't be 100 percent balanced. This means that you at least ask the bureaucrats to explain themselves. If they refuse, that's a different matter. But you shouldn't bypass this procedure. Professionalism is manifested not by specializing in reporting intense, deep-seated hatred, but in whether you can grasp the causes—what's behind it and why?

In 2002–2003, I studied social anthropology at Cambridge University under a U.K. scholarship. There are interesting similarities between anthropology and journalism: Both journalists and anthropologists have to live with their subjects, observe them closely, and be part of their lives. A substantial difference is that an anthropologist writes a thesis, which may be boring and only reach a small circle, while a reporter tells stories to a wide audience.

Journalists are messengers. Our mission is to highlight events in this complicated world, to help readers learn things beyond their own doors, beyond their own families, beyond their own boundaries, to expand their horizons. We're also like helmsmen—if the society is like the *Titanic* and we're going to crash into something and sink, someone on alert should say, hey guys, watch out, play it safe. Right now, what kind of development does China need? Is it sustainable, or is it a bubble that sooner or later will collapse? We should send some warning.

A journalist must be a good storyteller, but not just an entertainer. We have to be serious thinkers, make sense of things and find the inner logic. Our stories need to provoke thought and invite readers to get involved in debates.

Sometimes I feel fatigued with all the burning issues in China today. I think many social problems can be traced to lack of transparency, lack of public participation, lack of functioning democratic mechanisms. The system still operates by rule of man, the will of the chief, and the standard of the bureaucrats, who want to cover up negatives instead of being honest and responsible to the people. Without solving these root causes, we will forever report such problems.

That's why we journalists are here. We must act as whistle-blowers, incessantly producing stories. Over time we can get weary. It means that we all know the causes of the problems and feel a kind of repetitiveness even if the topics seem to be changing.

I think about what's next for me. Some of my foreign friends see a need for more nuanced, relatively balanced books about China by insiders. Maybe a Chinese reporter who writes in a foreign language should write a book to express his deepest understanding of China as an insider. The greatest challenge would be how to start, how to face the whole of China!

· 4 ·

Gong Wen
龚 雯

People's Daily
人 民 日 报

$\mathscr{G}$ong Wen prides herself on reporting from the lowest strata of society to the top levels of policymaking. She covered one of the biggest economic stories of recent years, China's entry into the World Trade Organization. As she describes, working for the official organ of the Chinese Communist Party gives her unusual access. Although its circulation has dropped from more than seven million in the early 1980s to about three million today, *People's Daily* remains China's flagship newspaper. From the sloganeering of the Cultural Revolution, when it was singularly preeminent, to the current era of reforms and competition, the paper signals political trends while acting as an authoritative source of news. The combination of history, status, and resources poses particular challenges for its journalists; drawn from the ranks of the best trained and most talented, with a strong sense of professionalism, they also must have finely honed political sensitivities. In 2007, Gong Wen took a break from chronicling China's expanding engagement with the global system to spend a year as a visiting scholar at the University of Cambridge, where she hoped, she wrote in an e-mail, "to renew my knowledge, reinforce my health, brush up my skills and broaden my horizons."

Some journalists are born to be journalists, and I feel that was my destiny. It's like a short story by the woman author Liu Suola that was popular in the 1980s: "You Have No Choice." I was a strong student from elementary school on, won lots of awards in middle school, got excellent scores on the national college entrance exams, and could have chosen any college and any major, but since childhood I'd always wanted to become a journalist. I even thought about becoming a war reporter so that I could brave the forests of guns and hail of bullets. Books that influenced me included *The Glory and the Dream* by William Manchester, which I read at middle school, and *Red Star over China* by Edgar Snow. I didn't choose a smooth path that easily leads to success, but this path suits me best. Nothing excites me more than getting a rare interview opportunity or a good news topic.

I've been a reporter since July 1992—and now I have an opportunity to summarize my entire career! Traveling this road, I've always been in too much of a hurry to give serious thought to my professional experiences. Some graduate student interns at my paper told me when they met me: "Oh, Teacher Gong, when were little we read your stories!" In fact, I still am not much older than they are, but the way they put it made me realize that, alas, time really flies.

I was born in Anhui Province but grew up in Jiangsu Province. My father was a government functionary, and my mother was a technician. I'm an only child—I was born premature, but weighed a strapping 4.3 kilos; they say if I'd been full term I would have weighed more than 5 kilos! The year before I was to take the college exams, my father died. We'd had a deep spiritual bond and he'd encouraged me to be a journalist, so his death was a severe blow. At that time, in the 1980s, China had many fewer media organizations and journalists were highly admired—unlike now, when criticism has given rise to the saying "guard against fire, theft, and journalists."

Nowadays, high-scoring students swarm to finance and business. Then, many high achievers wanted to study journalism. I'd always told everyone that I would apply to study journalism at Fudan University in Shanghai and, sure enough, I got in. I started college in 1988. The department chair took me under his wing. My freshman year, journalism reform was a popular topic, and we would keep discussing it even after the dormitory lights were turned off. Everyone shared in a sense of social responsibility. I went back to Fudan recently for a centennial celebration. The campus was the same, but it seemed the people had completely changed. Students are concerned about very different things now.

When *People's Daily* established journalism scholarships at Fudan and also at Renmin University in Beijing, I had the honor of being named one of the first recipients: I was the youngest, and the only freshman, which required special approval. My junior year, I had an internship at *People's Daily*. I'd hoped to report on culture or to work for the overseas edition, but I was assigned to the economics department. Probably this was fate. Half a year into my internship, the economics department took a fancy to me and asked Fudan to transfer me there. Thus was I effortlessly assigned to *People's Daily*, China's number one newspaper. I was among the last batch of college gradates whose job assignments were taken care of by the state.

I've been very lucky, as if a mysterious divine force was helping me all along until I finally achieved my wish. Although I've certainly faced pressure and chagrin over the years, not to mention painstaking and tiring toil, my path has been fairly smooth, and I've never considered giving up.

People's Daily publishes sixteen pages on weekdays and eighteen pages on weekends, and doesn't plan further expansion. Its target readership is decision-makers, government officials, executives, experts, and scholars. In addition, our readers include individual subscribers, paying from their own pockets, who want to learn about state policies in a timely manner and trust the paper won't hype or exaggerate. *People's Daily* is like a state-owned enterprise, big and all-inclusive. After you read today's issue, you will have an overview of various kinds of news, including international news.

I have two areas of focus. At the macro level, I report on major events, the overall situation, and China's international status. My other approach takes the commoners' angle, looking at happiness, anger, sorrows, and joys of ordinary people.

An example of the latter is a 1997 feature story titled "Four Days Traveling with Pigs," which ran on page two of *People's Daily* as part of a series on unusual occupations. I'd chosen to look into livestock transporting. Every day, three trains left the mainland carrying live pigs, beef cows, and lambs to supply the Hong Kong and Macau markets. I got on train number 8453—to this day, I remember this number—in Jinhua, a communications hub in Zhejiang Province, and rode more than 1,600 kilometers south to Shenzhen. The trip would not take much time by plane, but on a slow-moving freight train, it took four full days. The train was shabby and poorly equipped. Two other women and I shared a freight car with ninety-eight huge hogs—half of them on either side of a plywood shed in the middle for the human escorts.

If accompanying hog cargo is not the dirtiest, smelliest, most tiring job in the world, it surely is one of them. It was a foul, stinking environment. I got a taste of the hardship this job involves. First was the stench—so bad that I threw up as soon as I got on board. Second, the pigs bellowed all the time and I hardly got any sleep. Third, you had to learn to eat amidst pig shit. The last barrier was the hard work. You had to overcome all four obstacles.

My story had four chapters: starting off, surmounting the challenges, finding sources of diversion to relieve the hard work, and, finally, the rebuffs I encountered afterwards. At the trip's end, when we reached Shenzhen's north railway station, I was saturated with hog stench. I bid goodbye to my companions and tried to hail a taxi to the hotel where I'd booked a room. The first driver who stopped asked me: Miss, could you take another one? I asked why and he said: You smell too bad, and, if I take you, nobody else will want to ride in my cab, so please understand. Four or five more refused me as well. Eventually I got into a taxi and threatened to complain to the authorities unless he took me, and he yielded. When I went to the hotel shop to get shampoo and soap, the salesgirl appeared disgusted and covered her nose with her hand. I sealed my dirty clothes in a bag, soaked in the tub for more than two hours, and put on about half a bottle of perfume trying to disguise the smell, but it still lingered.

Think about it: I did this for just a few days, but those women escort pigs for the people of Hong Kong to eat day in and day out. They have a strong sense of responsibility and bear that smell as a perpetual signature.

My story finished with the observation that life is a rough but song-filled journey. It caused quite a commotion. The leadership of the trains sent a letter of thanks to our newspaper, commenting that, although the three freight trains had been operating for thirty-five years, I was the first reporter who'd ever gone along for the entire trip. Of course this praise might have been overdone. People are still writing me about how my story moved them to tears back in 1997. But this is the kind of attention I like to pay to ordinary people.

An example of my macro-level reporting is my work on China's admission into the World Trade Organization. Through the 1990s, I followed China's return to the world tariff and trade regime, which evolved into the WTO negotiations. I have broad contacts with key figures in the trade talks and have consulted voluminous data, so I know the whole process well—the key junctures, the benefits and costs. I got exclusive interviews with U.S. trade representatives and three WTO secretary-generals. I was the only reporter allowed at the conclusion of the Sino-U.S. bilateral agreement on WTO and the first to release news of its signing, and I also saw the signing of the Sino-European Union bilateral agreement.

In November 2001, the Chinese government was forming a delegation to go to Doha, Qatar, where a resolution was to be passed on China's admission into the WTO. Since I'd been covering the story all along, I wanted to be there. The Chinese government granted me special approval to go with the delegation as the only journalist member. Of course this also represented a kind of honor and trust for my newspaper. I got to sit in the second row of the conference hall at the gavel opening of the live broadcast ceremony—at 6:39 p.m. on the evening of November 10, 2001. It was the lead story, with an editorial, and *People's Daily* also gave me a whole page of precious space to review China's efforts to enter the WTO over the previous fifteen years.

Although I was made a member of the delegation, my main job was still reporting. I wrote for *People's Daily*, for its website people.com.cn, for the overseas edition, and for two other papers it publishes, *Huanqiu Shibao* (*Global Times*) and *Jinghua Shibao* (*Capital Times*). I also did reports for other papers. I wrote nonstop, sent out more than 100,000 characters in five or six days, and slept only three hours a day. It was definitely overwork. But I feel very happy about the experience and the fact that, other than some photojournalists, I was the only reporter at the scene to witness a historic moment.

I continue to cover WTO, and attended the most recent session in Hong Kong, again as a specially approved member of the Chinese delegation. I also helped them draft news releases and prepare some written materials. I have excellent relations with negotiators for the Chinese side; they trust me and have given me exclusive interviews.

The negotiations and agreements have their detractors, and the conference in Hong Kong was no exception. Korean farmers held demonstrations and clashed with police. This is normal and understandable, but I think grievances should be addressed through peaceful means, not through violence. Our focus is on China's interests and China's stand in the negotiations. As for demonstrations and parades and so on, we pay attention to them, and we also have our own critical view, but we reflect these aspects in the form of internally circulated reference reports.

Within China, controversy over WTO has abated, but a few years ago, about the time China joined, there were heated debates. There were two main factions: One thought the benefits would outweigh the costs, while the other thought the opposite, or that there would be no benefits at all. As a reporter who has followed the whole thing, I came to my own conclusion that, for China as a whole, benefits outweigh costs. My reporting proceeds from this standpoint and emphasizes the overall situation. Only through incessant opening up can the country blend into the waves of globalization and take its place—if not, it will become an isolated island and get left behind. Just think about it: 150 countries are members of WTO. If it were not a beneficial organization, why would everyone strive to get in?

To stay at *People's Daily*, I broke up with my first boyfriend. He was an outstanding science student. He went to the United States in the 1980s to study business. When I'd just started working at *People's Daily*, he made a trip back to China to tell me he wanted to take me to America. By then, he was pretty well settled and had his green card. I asked him: What can I do in America? Can I find a job at a major news organization like the one I currently have? If not, what else can I do? I have no desire to do anything else. He said: You can go back to school and then pursue some other profession or find a job with a corporation. I said no. He returned to America. We broke up and lost contact. I know he kind of hated me. It was I who proposed parting. He felt it inconceivable that I would give him up to be a journalist. But he may not have known how much I loved journalism. I've thought about these things often over the years, but I've never felt the slightest twinge of regret. I feel that having a career I enjoy in this blundering, harebrained era is happiness.

It's hard for me to identify challenges in my work, because I find being a journalist a great pleasure. I have a strong sense of professionalism, I grasp even unfamiliar subjects quickly, and I write fast—people have nicknamed me "quick hand." What might take others a week to finish takes me only a night, so I often get urgent jobs. I can assume heavy burdens as if they were light. In essence, I'm an optimist. I like fun and have a wide range of interests, so no matter how busy I get, I try to find time to do other things. I am devoted, responsible, earnest—but I'm not a workaholic or a writing machine. A veteran editor once told me journalists should go for coffee, attend concerts and the theater, and travel. Such activities intensify your powers of discovery, heighten your senses, and help you write more vividly. That is how I feel.

Main annoyances would be administrative tasks. Once leaders show their trust in you by promoting you, even to a minor position such as section leader or editor, you have to bother with trivialities. For instance, I had to attend a work conference this morning that had nothing to do with news. Such things divert time and energy from reporting, writing, pondering stories, and discovering news leads. I'd like to be a pure journalist, a pure newswoman, without so many disturbances.

What most gratifies me is the recognition I've gained. The newspaper has recognized my work: I got promoted to associate senior editor in 1999 and to senior editor in 2005, each time as the youngest at that rank. I've won many awards, including a national news award three times. I've lost count of how many of my stories were republished by foreign media, how many were praised by leaders at various levels, how many produced relatively strong social repercussions. Nor can I count the letters and calls I've received from enthusiastic readers. These things don't make me complacent or give me a swelled head; on the other hand, they make me sure of myself and confident that my efforts are worthwhile.

In December 2003, I was covering a national conference on business affairs at which Vice Premier Wu Yi, the former minister of foreign trade, was making a speech. All of a sudden, she asked: Is Gong Wen here? I was sitting in the back row and stood up. She said: Do you all know about the article by famous reporter Gong Wen of *People's Daily* titled "A Calm and Temperate Look at Trade Frictions"?

Various factions in China were debating the increase in trade frictions, and some wondered whether joining WTO had brought more trouble to China.

I didn't have any special materials on the issue, nor had anyone indoctrinated me as to what viewpoint I should hold. I drew my own conclusions through research and observation: When trade volume increases, trade frictions will also increase. This is a normal phenomenon. Japan and the U.S. are allies, but they still have trade wars. The same is true with the EU and the U.S. When a similar thing occurs with China, people too easily get startled or alarmed. So I wrote this article, and it ran on the front page of *People's Daily* and caused a stir.

Wu Yi suggested everyone read this article. After the conference, she called me over and joked: Look, I acted as a salesperson for your article today. You should pay me a kickback! Such recognition gives me a sense of accomplishment.

Compared to other jobs, a journalist's work is always fresh, as the sun is new every day. A journalist travels far and wide and sees all sides of the human condition. You get to be in the front row to witness and record history. You can participate in the development and changes of the times. You also are relatively free of the sort of rigid rules and strict hierarchy found in government departments or big corporations. Some of my classmates became government officials. They are enjoying their incomes and benefits and climbing the ladder step by step. Some of my college classmates have gone into business. They earn more money than me, and tell me that with my abilities and intelligence I surely would be very successful in business. I tell them I think I'll stick with journalism.

Chinese journalists, especially reporters for central news organizations such as Xinhua or *People's Daily*, have low incomes. Many reporters at my paper are outstanding graduates of the best universities. If they went to work elsewhere, they could make a very comfortable living. They chose this profession because they love it. But the profession doesn't reward them with corresponding compensation.

Reporters must stay independent. Once you have economic involvement with a story, you can hardly maintain independence. Every news organization in China has made it clear that "red envelopes"—payoffs for attending news conferences or things like that—are impermissible. *People's Daily* has problems, but not that: If a reporter accepts money, he can't be a reporter. Career finished. However, at many other news organizations, accepting red envelopes is tacitly allowed; if nobody reports on you, then that's the way it is. In fact, this is abnormal and at variance with the concepts we learned in journalism school.

When reporters travel to attend meetings, those who invite them often pay for their transportation and lodging. In China, many news organizations have low budgets for travel—probably one trip to Hainan Island would finish it up. So sponsors naturally think: I pay your expenses and you cover my conference. That's the way it works. But would you say anything that is not in their favor? Can you expose their problems? You can only report the good side and the false show of peace and prosperity.

I think the status of journalists in China is declining. When I entered the career in 1992, journalists for organizations like *People's Daily* and Xinhua got tremendous respect. These brand names still carry weight, but it's not like a decade or two ago when people would turn to media to reflect problems or convey grievances. The change is understandable; with more outlets and increased competition, some media hunt for novelty, grab scoops, and resort to hype. But it makes me uneasy. My personal opinion is that many Chinese journalists are in fact very idealistic, capable, and hardworking, especially those who graduated from college in the 1980s and early 1990s. They deserve respect and trust.

Now there are many more media voices, and people can choose different media according to their own desires to access news and understand the world. I hope media will become even more manifold and open. Whether we call it propaganda or communication, our attitudes and viewpoints should be calm and even-handed.

A Chinese saying goes: You cannot recognize the true face of Mount Lushan from within the mountains. People who live in this society are experiencing gradual change unknowingly. Because of the focus of my reporting, I can feel the steady opening up to the outside world due to the deepening of the reforms. I feel happy about it. Ten or more years ago, whenever Chinese went abroad, everything seemed novel and we wanted to buy this and that, even though we didn't have much money. Nowadays when we go abroad, we've neither much need nor desire to buy things. I went abroad several times this year and my purse is much fuller than ten years ago, but I did very little shopping because basically I could get everything at home. This is a huge change.

Those of us who are immersed in our work tend to forget that our energies are limited. I feel the need to get reenergized through further study. I also want to organize materials I've gathered over the years and write one or two worthwhile books. I've accumulated a lot of stuff that couldn't be published through regular channels, including inside stories about China joining the WTO, but sooner or later it will no longer be confidential, and I'm waiting for that day. Over the years, I've also met people I admire and respect for the roles they played in promoting China's reform, opening up, social progress, and development. I want to write about them, perhaps a couple of biographies.

I'm not in a position to give advice to young journalists; each generation has its own concepts and ways of making a living. I'd just say you must truly love journalism, or you'll get weary and won't derive pleasure from it.

When I was a student, my teachers emphasized that facts are the lifeblood of journalism. I agree this is fundamental. You can be flexible about many things, but you should never bend on this. It is the bottom line.

Frequently what we see and hear and think we know is far from the truth, so journalists not only need to record, but also must think and discern. One of my principles is never to parrot others. Another is to refrain from fads or hype. I might not be the earliest with a story, but I'm more accurate and comprehensive; I'd rather stay half a beat slower for the sake of truth and facts.

Joseph Pulitzer said something I copied down the other day, about a nation being like a ship sailing on the sea with journalists watching from the prow for unpredictable winds and clouds and submerged reefs and shoals, and providing timely warning. My strongest desire is to be there when important news breaks out, and to convey it at once as comprehensively, objectively, and accurately as possible.

We also should help society progress. The Chinese say journalists should bear morality and justice on their iron shoulders as they write fine articles with their delicate hands. Our shoulders are still not as strong as iron. Competition is intense, and some media simply cater to popular taste. Reporters should have social responsibility and humanistic passion—as a line of poetry puts it, rivers and mountains on all sides in my eyes, sorrow and happiness of ten thousand families in my heart. Journalists should aspire to reporting that withstands the trial of time and leaves its wake in the long river of history. A journalist should keep one eye on today and another on the future.

・ 5 ・

Tan Hongkai
谭 宏 凯

China Daily
中 国 日 报

As opinions editor of *China Daily*, Tan Hongkai belongs to a corps of distinctively positioned mediators between East and West. Six days a week, a mostly Chinese staff produces this national English-language paper. Soft-spoken, modest, with an <u>understated</u> streak of humor and a boyish visage, Tan landed there after taking a recruitment test as a <u>lark.</u> He depicts himself as a journeyman trying his best; he's emphatic that his title carries little authority, although inquiries around the newsroom reveal that he's highly respected. *China Daily*, launched in 1981 as growing numbers of foreigners were arriving in China, targets tourists and <u>expatriate</u> readers and also is read by many Chinese. Its circulation is said to be around 200,000; the organization also runs a lucrative stable of educational weeklies in English for Chinese students. The daily paper is government backed and sometimes construed as an official voice, although its journalists don't see themselves that way. Many staffers have overseas experience, including Tan, who took a year off from the paper to study journalism at Stanford University. Tan was born in March 1965. In the spring of 2007, a University of Iowa exchange program with *China Daily* brought him to Iowa for a month to teach, his first experience up front in the classroom.

～

I became a journalist through an odd combination of circumstances.

I majored in philosophy at Sichuan University. My English was pretty good and I followed foreign media reports on China as a college undergraduate—in the late 1980s, there were few channels, but I read almost every issue of *Time* and *Newsweek*.

I earned a master's degree in political science from Jilin University, and faced several options for employment upon graduation—working for a petroleum company, a central government agency, or a university. I really had no interest in going to a central government department, so my adviser recommended me for a teaching position at Xiamen University. I'd never been to Xiamen but what I knew about the place sounded good; plus, as a special economic zone, it was likely to have a relaxed atmosphere. I decided to take this job. The university had even arranged my teaching schedule.

In early 1989, my final winter vacation before going to Xiamen, I spent two months in Beijing, staying with a friend who worked for *Guangming Daily* and had heard that *China Daily* was recruiting. "Doesn't everyone say your English is good?" my friend teased me. "Everyone's applying to *China Daily*. If you're really talented, you should give it a try."

So for fun, I took a recruiting test. I truly had no intentions of working for *China Daily*; it was just a joke between friends. I didn't even apply for a journalism position because the other applicants were English majors. I merely took the test and took off, and never bothered to learn the results.

As I was about to leave Beijing, my friend taunted me: "Such a brat, you took their test but didn't dare find out your score!" So I called *China Daily*—I hadn't left them any contact information—and they told me to come over right away. The two editors who were interviewing candidates said I'd done a fine job on the test and asked if I'd like to work for them.

I thought I might as well give it a try. It's been sixteen years.

Initially, *China Daily* wanted me to work in the sports department, which was short-handed. I didn't want to work in sports. An opinions editor was interested in my academic background, so I went to that department.

As neither a student of journalism nor an English major, I faced a transition. Once I'd adapted to the foreign-language environment, I took the initiative to do some newsgathering, and senior comrades gave me advice and help. I covered news related to legal and administration reforms in China, and I learned through experience.

China Daily's opinion page has undergone some changes over the past few years, although personally I think they've been minor. One positive change is that the paper now runs editorials every day.

China Daily used to think editorials had to focus on major events, such as central government meetings; only then would something be worth an editorial.

There were no designated editorial writers—instead, when the editorial board thought it necessary to comment on a big event, they would choose a senior person to write it. Actually, they didn't even have the confidence to call it an editorial, which implies we have valuable views. Senior editors would say, "This is our commentary." Later, the editorial board decided a newspaper couldn't do without editorials. So we got editorials, and involved more people, although there still was no fixed list of editorial writers. Eventually, they decided to have editorials every day. For a time, we ran three editorials a day, but members of the editorial board thought that was too many. Now we generally publish two.

Even before we started daily editorials, I'd been thinking and talking with my colleagues about how to create our page and improve our process. I proposed that every morning we gather to talk about the day's news leads and discuss potential subjects of editorials, which might or might not ultimately get published. Others questioned the necessity of doing this, or whether we could stick to it once we started. But we persisted. Each day, we determine the subjects for the next day's editorials. If there is anything I feel good about, it would be this.

Every morning at 9:30, several people convene in my office. First, everyone talks about what's in the news that might be worth writing about. We list the stories, discuss their importance, choose two subjects, and brainstorm about the issues and what angles to take. Then I ask who can write these and assign the writing tasks. Actual publication is up to the senior editors. I personally don't make the final decisions regarding editorials—if I could, it wouldn't be right. I'm not even a member of *China Daily*'s editorial board. The editorials represent the institution. So it should not be me. I don't have any objection.

It's hard to single out a specific article as noteworthy, but we had some fine articles on the U.S. going to war in Iraq. I think we did a good job following such a major event. Our opinions page on the start of the Iraq war didn't please the U.S. Embassy. A cartoon we ran—which had nothing to do with me—hit a nerve, and they came to see us, saying *China Daily* had gone too far. Along with editorials, we ran commentaries by individuals, dealing with principles of international relations or issues of morality and justice. *China Daily*'s standpoint was that only when the UN's role was given full play and every means was exhausted could one resort to force. We weren't anti-American, as the embassy charged; we simply presented the views of this media outlet.

We make relatively independent decisions as an organization; our opinions are entirely ours—not directly tied up with official background, as we're often viewed, nor issued on someone else's instructions. We do not represent ourselves as a mouthpiece—other media may have that concept, but not us. On the Taiwan issue, say, we hope to stand between Taibei and Beijing and see exactly what's going on. Can we look at issues from the angle of a third party calmly, objectively, and rationally? We've done some good articles on Taiwan affairs in a certain phase. Now things are more complicated.

Our editorials cover quite a wide range. Yesterday, for instance, the Chinese Academy of Social Sciences issued its annual report analyzing social developments of the past year and making some forecasts for the next. People are especially concerned about what we call "the three difficulties"— costs of and access to medical care, housing, and education. So we chose this as one topic. Also, China just released third-quarter statistics on the gross domestic product under a new economic reporting system, but there are conflicts and inconsistencies in the statistics. The latest announcement had some changes in GDP rankings among the provinces and municipalities. Has Guangdong surpassed Shandong? What's Beijing's ranking? And Shanghai? This sort of discussion is going on. Not so long ago, everyone was saying China had been overemphasizing productivity while overlooking pollution and other social tolls. There was talk of "green GDP" as an index to measure development, taking into consideration social, human, and environmental criteria. Yet the provinces still compare numbers and hype GDP. So this was our second topic.

I was appointed deputy editor of the opinions department in 1994, and editor in 2001. In between, during 1997–1998, I spent a year at Stanford University. My time there gave me an understanding of U.S. and Western mainstream journalism concepts and broadened my vision. I also studied basic journalism techniques, which probably was of more direct and obvious benefit. I returned both more confident and more passionate. I also could write better.

My classmates at Stanford thought that, since then I had the title of deputy opinions editor, I must be a somebody, but things work differently in China. I don't control all the contents of this page. For instance, the chief editor selects the columnists. Our current chief editor, who started at the end of 2005, formed a commentary group with a regular roster of about seven people. He sometimes invites me to their meetings, but I do my work separately.

A long-term weakness at *China Daily* has to do with the nature of our knowledge. More than 90 percent of our journalists were language students. Most came directly from college, without life experience. Nor did they have specialized knowledge. Consider the staff of my opinions page. Most are in their twenties. For quite awhile, I've been the oldest one, although two slightly older people just got assigned to me. Even I find writing decent editorials hard.

In daily work, manpower is a troublesome issue. My biggest problem is that few people are both interested in this work and capable. Neither are my own abilities as good as I would like. I cannot cope with everything; as a result, each day I attend to some things and neglect others. Today, I dislike this part; tomorrow, I dislike that part; and often I find it's all no good.

Young people say that our "play" environment isn't good, by which they mean we don't have enough freedom. I agree with them. Everybody in China knows this. I discuss with my colleagues how we can do more. We try incessantly to move forward, and, in this respect, even one single step is better than empty talk. I'll ask myself: Have I exhausted all available possibilities? Maybe I haven't.

I think sometimes in our society, and in our vocation, we suffer from a kind of inertia. It's a practical question: Sometimes we simply haven't made enough effort. In fact, we can put certain issues on the table in China now. For instance, can you find a place without any censorship? No, it's everywhere. It's like human rights. My premise is these problems exist everywhere, only differing in modes and degrees. Talking about them is not that formidable.

On a higher level, I wonder how we can achieve a healthy consensus on the role of the media. Inside the media industry, we are striving for our ideal—freedom of the press, which we Chinese don't talk about. Meanwhile, how can media fulfill their social responsibility? Outside the industry, how can government best understand that more freedom for the media is good for society? Reaching consensus would improve our work, benefit society, and be easier for the leadership.

I think journalism anywhere should be based on social justice and impartiality, making contributions to society as well as taking responsibility in society. Whether you are capitalist or socialist or Marxist, journalists should have the same professional integrity. People may differ on specific issues and even stand on different philosophical ground, but members of this profession should share approximately the same core concepts and criteria for behavior.

We've seen huge changes in society and in our industry. Chinese society and Chinese media are no longer homogeneous. Reforms have brought changes with each passing year, and public consciousness has changed greatly. Chinese media saw a lot of activity in the 1980s; by the time I joined they were less active; and now it is difficult to say whether media are active or not. In terms of ownership, the changes have not been that especially great. But media continue to diversify. This is unstoppable. This is a great change. And I believe this process will have direct impact on market structures when China truly has market-driven media in the future.

It's difficult to make predictions five or ten years down the road. This is because, under our system, things happen beyond the will of any particular individuals or groups. I do think media diversification has just begun, and that more mature media with distinctive personalities will emerge. As for what I hope will happen, I hope to see more, faster, and more active changes. The government says it wants to build a harmonious society, which will be difficult unless the media have sufficient space. At the same time, media organizations and journalists must make better use of this space and freedom. We must be mindful of our responsibilities to earn the public trust.

Over the years, I've heard young people say they want to go into journalism because every day will be fresh and each assignment exciting. Curiosity is an important basic condition for being a good journalist. But curiosity isn't enough. You should ask yourself if you are willing to sacrifice personal interests, and even your life, for this cause. The job won't necessarily be what you expect. It won't always bring fame and gain. It has its own pressures and problems. Can you bear it? Are you willing to bear it? Becoming a journalist is like making a serious promise, to do the job well enough and for the long haul.

To put it another way, if you want to make money, you should work for a corporation. There may be a better place for you than journalism. Once you jump in, you must be able to face it.

A benefit of being a journalist is getting to go places you want to go and see things you want to see because of your work. I've studied Western philosophy and sociology and political science and a hodgepodge of things, and—although I consider officialdom sordid and boring—I'm interested in politics and social issues. I feel a newsman in a developing society like China should feel happy, even with all the problems.

What I do isn't anything to brag about. All I can say is that I've done my best in many things most of the time. Looking back, probably much of my work concerns petty matters. But I feel that if we pay attention to these matters and readers think what we've written is good, then we've done a good job.

· *6* ·

Jin Yongquan
晋 永 权

China Youth News
中 国 青 年 报

*D*uring his graduate studies in Marxist theory, Jin Yongquan made an un-likely detour into journalism. Beginning as an intern and rising to the ranks of upper editors at the daily *China Youth News*, he continues to write and do photography. He's published two books on projects dovetailing with his report-ing work, and a third on Chinese photojournalism. Pluck and stubbornness, along with luck and circumstance, seem to have served him well. While mak-ing the most of opportunities his unanticipated career provides, he's learned from accommodating mentors and been insulated by protective supervisors. *China Youth News*, official organ of the Chinese Communist Youth League and published since 1951, claims a circulation of half a million. It was one of the first papers in China to start an online edition. Generally a more relaxed and flexible workplace than other media at this top tier of national publications, the daily or one of its ancillary publications occasionally oversteps bounds, top editors get replaced, and others carry on.

I grew up in Anhui Province; my father was a middle school teacher who got transferred frequently, from this city to that, or from city to countryside, so I just followed. After I became a journalist, he commented that I was still running around, never staying in one place for long. Perhaps it has to do with my childhood experiences.

I was the fourth of six kids. The Chinese put a lot of emphasis on family. But as number four with older brothers and sisters above and younger ones below, I fell into the category where I could almost escape my parents' attention. The older siblings shouldered more responsibility, while the younger ones needed to be cared for. I was relatively free; from early on I felt I could do anything I liked.

Originally, my studies had nothing to do with journalism or photojournalism. I went to a teacher's vocational school and then a teacher's college in Hefei, the provincial capital, and studied English and political science. In the late 1980s, Chinese society was undergoing drastic ideological changes. I was muddleheaded about many issues, but wanted to get to the bottom of them—so I applied to a special place for graduate school, the Marxism Development Research Institute at Renmin University. By now I've almost forgotten its full name and just call it the Marx-Lenin Institute; I had to look up the long name this morning. This institute was one of seventeen set up nationwide after the founding of the People's Republic in 1949 to study the theoretical transmission of Marxism in China from a historical perspective. I enrolled in 1990, and my strict training in Marxist classic theories commenced.

My father taught politics, and when I was in primary school I'd looked at some of his books. Young boys love books about war, and I clearly remember taking Marx's *The Civil War in France* off the shelf and starting to read. I couldn't understand it. I thought to myself: Here's a book on war—why I can't understand it? It was a shocking discovery. Why did it have such a title but no pictures—no swords and guns? I took down a book called *How Lenin Studies*. It was beyond my comprehension. Why didn't it tell me how Lenin learned by heart, how he wrote, and how he dealt with teachers? Nothing. There wasn't anything I could understand. When I passed the exams to get into the Marx-Lenin Institute and went for my interview, I said I hoped to find answers to all the books and questions that I hadn't understood as a child. The teachers burst into laughter.

In the midst of my graduate studies, a great deal happened. The Soviet Union disintegrated and disavowed Marxism, and Eastern Europe saw a series of changes as well. These events had even greater impact on me than my previous ignorance. Book knowledge suddenly short-circuited in my mind. I remained perplexed.

Adjacent to my classmates and me in the dorm lived graduate students in journalism. They looked down on us. They told us: The USSR has fallen apart. You Marxism students are finished! We likewise had a dim view of their field:

Journalism wasn't a serious field of scholarship. So we talked about history, ideology, and theory, and had good communication and interaction on these topics. The journalism students influenced us. Whether we influenced them, only they know.

I got a chance to visit Russia, and what I saw there sharply contrasted with what I'd read. I was shocked. This is when I decided to find a journalism job. That would be a better route to understanding reality and finding out the truth.

Nonetheless, I earnestly completed my graduate program. I was, in the school's view, an outstanding Communist Party member, an outstanding student leader, a scholarship winner. I could have gone to a job at a state agency writing theoretical articles, or working as a Party secretary for central leaders, enjoying good benefits. But I'd chosen to be a journalist, even if the income and social status are not among the highest. Of course, when you plunge into something, you discover plenty of problems and things that fail to match your expectations.

During my final year in graduate school, through an introduction from another student, I got an internship in the photo department of *China Youth News*. This is a relatively nonbureaucratic newspaper, and a good place for young people since promotion does not depend on seniority. The photo director was the well-known photojournalist He Yanguang. He asked me: Have you ever studied journalism? I said no. Have you ever studied photography? No again. Have you heard of He Yanguang? I said I hadn't. He said okay, you may be an intern here. As a matter of fact, I'd studied some journalism history and theory and borrowed a lot of books on journalism, I'd done photography in middle school, and I knew of He Yanguang. Why did I answer no? It was a small stratagem—not knowing as much as journalism students, I might as well plead ignorance! Evidently He Yanguang thought it was a good thing.

The second day of my internship, more than one hundred photos arrived in the mail. Director He told me to select ten publishable pictures. So I chose ten and did some cropping and wrote captions. Then he asked me to select three out of the ten. I did. He said fine and signed off. From that time on, he couldn't care less about this routine; I would forge his signature to approve pictures for publication and send them to the main editorial office. He never authorized me—it just happened, things muddled along, everyone doing what had to be done. It was heady: a mere intern given the right to decide the fate of so many pictures!

A few months later, when I visited the photo department of Asahi News of Japan and presented my business card, which had the title "photo editor," they showed unusual respect and surprise that I was an editor at such a young age. In fact, our editors were equivalent to secretaries, or office boys.

During my internship, I applied for jobs at other newspapers. One agreed to take me and told me to get ready. One day the chief editor of that paper saw He Yanguang and asked him: How is our *Xiao Jin*—young Jin—doing at your place? He Yanguang said: *Your* Xiao Jin? How has he become your Xiao Jin? The editor told him about my job there. When He returned to the office, he told me not to look elsewhere, just to stay. This was around the end of 1992. After graduating, I formally joined the *China Youth News* staff in July 1993.

I'm always thinking about fighting against the fragility and evanescence of journalism. All the little items a journalist writes everyday, and the news photos. What's the purpose? Why do this?

What makes me happiest is to be able to do serious and enduring reporting. I usually make long-term plans. I've completed two five-year plans. The first covered 1995–2000, during which I reported on a kind of Han subculture in villages in the border area of Fujian and Jiangxi provinces in southeastern China. I focused on rural religious activities and customs involving mask dancing and exorcism that have a history of over eight hundred years. Our newspaper ran six of my reports, and the project culminated in a book with my photographs, written with two younger colleagues, called *The Last Hans*.

It started when a colleague from the advertising department asked me to go with him on a business trip. I was happy to go—someone else was paying and I could sightsee. In Linchuan, Jiangxi Province, he went out to discuss money and ads and I visited former residences of a prime minister and a famous playwright and went to museums. I noticed a picture on a billboard, soggy from rain, and asked local people what this mask dancing was about. They weren't clear, so they found me an expert.

Mask dancing practices had stopped during the Cultural Revolution and were revived in the late 1970s. The main rituals are held during the lunar new year and usually last eighteen days. I spent five Spring Festival holidays down there and other occasions as well. My longest stay was thirty-eight days. In the process, my professional roles blurred; I didn't feel like a pure journalist, but rather like an anthropologist, taking field notes, collecting artifacts, and doing research.

It just so happened that the first time I went down for the holidays was right after my wedding. My wife is in banking, and she also moved around quite a bit. We had a half-joking, half-serious talk. I told her: Now that you are married to a reporter, you should comfort yourself that I am not going to a war zone. She said: Okay, you can go. Another year she was considering going along, on the condition that she could take a bath. When she travels for her work, she stays at five- or four-star hotels, and needs to bathe and drink tea and so on. I said it wouldn't be possible to take a bath for at least half a month. If she couldn't bear that, we could go to the county seat, but the road is so bumpy that if you leave the village you won't want to come back, and if you return to the village you won't want to leave again. After hearing this, she gave up and left me alone.

Reporting from the countryside made me understand a plain truth—that when it comes to social relations in China, if you can open one link in a chain, it becomes possible to open all the links. For example: I meet you and cultivate a good relationship. You trust me and invite me to your home. For Chinese New Year, I bring you cartons of cigarettes and a couple of bottles of liquor. The next day you take me to your maternal uncle's home, and your uncle takes me to his sister's, and the sister to her paternal uncle's. Thus the whole rural chain opens up. So you must be sincere and very nice to the first person you meet. If you offend him, you may ruin everything that could follow. Even in urban society, sometimes we have to act this way. Say you want to interview someone, it's much more productive to get to know the interviewee through friends than through official assignment and formal arrangement.

Working as a journalist, I'd done many things casually, and some were just propaganda. People invited you over. They paid for your train ride or airfare. You stayed in hotels. They paid for your meals. Everything was paid for. In the case of this project, I took it on regardless of any consideration. I spent a lot of time on travel and each time I emphasized a different angle. I stayed with one particular family frequently, and helped my landlady prepare documents for a lawsuit against the local government over the contract for an orchard and a fishpond, which I wrote about in one report. Her home was my central beachhead, from which I'd cover an area radiating out several dozen kilometers. Often more than ten people would accompany me: Some carried my boxes, my tripod, my cameras. We looked like British colonial anthropologists with their entourage of hired locals marching into the hinterlands of Asia. Of course I didn't need to hire anyone; we were already good friends. I never had to worry about meals or where to stay the night; relatives everywhere would take us in.

The Chinese character for the mask dancing ritual is ancient and hard to write. Many people don't recognize it. Others think the topic is insignificant or that villages are uninteresting. At first there wasn't much reaction to my reports in *China Youth News*. Some people were suspicious. Was it religion? Religious themes sometimes can't be reported on. But to me the subject was fascinating. It plays both historic and contemporary roles in religion and politics—in fact, the structure of administration and religion works as one in these villages. Eight people perform the rituals, and behind them are thirty-two headmen from the major families who orchestrate important matters in the villages. Finally my articles began evoking interest. The subject connects with people's nostalgia about the past. The Han are the largest ethnic group in China but now have few distinctive ethnic characteristics, whether in dress or in beliefs.

They wear Western suits. My project showed cultural distinctiveness among people who are Han, which is why I called the book *The Last Hans*.

In 2000, I started my second major project, on the Three Gorges migration. The Chinese government planned to move a total of 1.28 million people out of the area to be flooded for the Three Gorges hydroelectric project. Over four years, I followed the involuntary relocation of 166,000 migrants to other provinces. It began on August 13, 2000, when the first batch left Nanxi Town in Chongqing municipality for Chongming Island in Shanghai municipality. By August 29, 2004, the task had been completed.

I went on sixteen trips to report on the migration, the longest lasting four weeks, and produced more than sixteen articles for my paper. Our management is quite loose, which means more latitude. So what were the preconditions? I have a month to go out shooting pictures—I did this project in black and white. The newspaper pays travel expenses and the cost of film. As long as I do a page for the paper upon my return, everything will be okay.

The headline for my first report in the paper was "Tearful Departure from the Three Gorges." It drew a severe reprimand: The central propaganda department issued a circular to our paper and other media organizations, saying the migrants had left their hometown happily and willingly. Why did you describe them as tearful? Why did you have only one color picture? At that time the U.S. movie *Schindler's List* was being shown and I kind of imitated the scene with the little girl in a red coat. I arranged a whole page of black-and-white pictures, except for one little girl in a column of immigrants wearing yellow-patterned clothing and holding a puppy in her arms. She was the only one with color.

I'm a journalist, not a propagandist. That's why I got criticized. Knowing the leadership of the paper was under pressure from above, I requested time off for the next trip. I'd be photographing a climactic episode, migration on a larger scale, the longest trip of all. This batch would go by bus to the banks of a branch of the Yangtze River, then transfer to a big boat that would carry them down the Yangtze to Yichang, where they would board a train, and after that more bus rides. Altogether it would take them six days to reach Huizhou in Guangdong Province. I had to go. I asked for leave to travel at my own expense. The leaders said never mind, just go, consider it half travel and half newsgathering, you can take pictures of landscape and scenery. Of course scenery is not news, so it wouldn't get published. By the time I returned, perhaps they had forgotten. I filed another major report on the big migration.

I discovered that, having criticized you once, officials will find it awkward to criticize you again. They can't keep scolding you all the time. They didn't even criticize a piece I wrote called "Notes on Leaving the Three Gorges" with exclusive information, including news of accidents during the migration such as vehicles flipping over and people killed. The bottom line of the bottom line was truth. I wouldn't accept hearsay; if I hadn't reported it or witnessed it myself, I wouldn't put it in my articles. Along with pictures, I had hard and fast interview notes and sometimes voice recordings to back up my stories.

I wrote most of my book, about 90,000 characters, in three months. Just this morning, Sanlian Publishing House asked me to check the cover. I wanted to make an individual record of this great migration, and took lots of notes. However, when I started the book, I resolutely avoided my notes—some from a year ago, some from three years ago, still others from five years ago. I wrote about the things that could make me remember; I figured that if I couldn't recall something, it must not have moved me, and wouldn't move readers. Only after I finished the draft did I go back to my notes to check the facts—names of people and places, statistics—and make necessary factual corrections.

One chapter describes how a country girl left home and became a child prostitute and then took part in the migration. I met her on a migration boat. She bought a house for her parents at her new settlement, but her parents gave up the house to return to their hometown. The girl had gone from vagrant to migrant. Now her identity was linked to the state, and she thought she could find help somewhere.

The ease of publication was a great surprise to me. I'd thought such a sensitive subject would have to wait many years. Nobody even touched my text except for some typos and stylistic changes. The title is *Out of the Three Gorges*. Some people asked me if it was a reference to the bible story "Out of Egypt," and I told them read it yourself.

What I learned from this project is that, if you persevere, opportunities will flow to you. If something's important enough, stick with it. By my fourth or fifth trip, whenever events related to the Yangtze River or the Three Gorges arose, such as cutting into the river to build the dam, the editors would come to me and say: Hey, how come you're still here? You should get going tomorrow! It was no longer a question of who might approve my trip or who'd pay for it, it was: Hurry up, go whatever way you like, take a plane!

Probably I was able to carry this project so far because people ultimately accepted my stubbornness as my strength. This story belongs to you; you know what boat to take even with your eyes closed. And who else would want to go? Others might want to be sent to Shanghai, or Shenzhen, or Hong Kong. And if there's any chance for Tokyo, let me go! But for this, the leadership can't find anyone else. There's only this one guy who, in the hottest season of July and August, wants to go. This fool is willing to live with peasants at a five-yuan-a-day hostel. He's willing to eat their melons and drink river water and bad liquor. Let him go!

In truth, I'm not in the best of shape, and I, too, would like staying in fancy hotels and swimming and taking baths and enjoying the sea and the sunshine.

But I didn't consider these trips hardships. On the contrary, this mission made me very happy. Deep down, I knew exactly what I was going to do and why.

He Yanguang is now chief photo supervisor, and I became head of the photo department half a year ago, so I do less reporting. The biggest challenge is how to organize others to gather news and take pictures, and how to better approach the truth while also avoiding pitfalls, both professional and political. In fact, sometimes my work involves helping younger reporters accomplish these things.

After my first two years in the photo department, I spent five years in the general editorial office as a front-page editor. The work included text editing, page layout, and selecting and organizing pictures. Working nights taught me about requirements from above—what can be reported and what can't, how to deal with the leadership. So I have an understanding of journalism operations. Reporting is reporting. The key thing is to handle it well and minimize the risks.

For example, I wrote an editor's note in today's paper to accompany a page of pictures of international graffiti at the Great Wall. It touches on two sensitive questions. I refer to graffiti carved by someone from "a certain southeast Asian country" dated December 17, 2005, four days ago. Our reporter knows it was a Malaysian tourist. Naming the country might cause tensions in the relationship between China and Malaysia. There's also graffiti in Arabic, which I don't understand. Maybe it's just someone's name, maybe it's a sentence, I don't know. Still we published it. If this picture is questioned, I can say my knowledge is limited and I don't read many foreign languages.

As a journalist in my thirties, I have survived my bold and immature twenties and wish to keep my career going longer and better into my forties and fifties. Another challenge is choosing what *not* to do. Temptations come up in great numbers: You publish something for me and I'll give you some benefits. You might get three phone calls a day asking you to do three things. Can you find good excuses to decline two? Sorry, I don't feel well today and can't go to dinner with you. Sorry, I cannot take three hours for a meal, I have a page to finish. I'm tied up at work, so I can't make it to the party this evening and will be unable to get the gifts you prepared. In reality, this is somewhat hard to do.

Once a colleague from another newspaper complained to me about his wife scolding him for eating out every day. I asked him how many meals he ate out. He said five meals a day on average. How long does each take? Including drinks and recovery from the dizziness, usually three hours. That would add up to fifteen hours! If you include sleeping, what time is left for work? What's happened to your ideals and your profession as a journalist?

I've been a journalist for twelve years, and for at least the first eight I puzzled over the difference between news and propaganda. Sometimes propaganda could be turned into news; for instance, a certain place would invite you to a fiftieth anniversary celebration, with good food, good hotel, good cars, in the interests of generating propaganda, but you'd find the celebration wasteful and ordinary people fenced out, which would be news.

You must be clear about your job. If you are responsible for propaganda, then your responsibilities should be propagating the wishes and requirements of a specific principal party—the boss of a company, the top leader of a unit, a department head, or a university president. Usually the principal party wants his message spread through magnification: Our school has the most beautiful new building, with the best labs, and our faculty are the best dressers. Other messages must be shrunk: We don't have enough teachers, and our teachers have only master's degrees, not doctorates, and some have bogus degrees. If someone asks about these questions, we will try our best to minimize them down to zero. This is propaganda. Journalism, on the contrary, tries to maximize that zero: This university hardly has any real professors, many don't have diplomas, and some have fake ones. That's journalism.

In reality, we still meet many practical difficulties in differentiating between the two. We are managed by the central propaganda department, which has many requirements for newspapers under its supervision. Various interest groups also have influence on your newspaper. In the past, government was the largest interest group; now it's business, as well as other nongovernmental forces. Finally, the journalist regulates himself. In deciding to report something or not, we apply self-discipline, and maybe forgo or just simplify the story. Should *The New York Times* report that Bush is monitoring foreign visitors and those with Middle East contacts? Maybe not when the war against terror is still going on. Maybe we can wait two more years until Bush steps down. In effect, such self-discipline is injurious to the profession. Ultimately you may end up doing things you don't want to do.

I think that, of all the principles for journalism, the most important is to complicate simple things and simplify complicated things. At first sight, you may think something is simple, but it may conceal a great deal. However, in facing a very complex thing, you should find out its essence. What is the key to this event? Why is it so? The United States cites all kinds of excuses for attacking Iraq—but which are decisive? Bush's personal character? Oil?

As for other principles, truth is fundamental. If you are not allowed to speak, you can stay silent, or laugh. But you shouldn't tell lies. Discerning truth is not simple. Chinese society is undergoing drastic changes, and polarization between wealthy and poor has reached an extreme. Those with power, money, and force can easily exert control over journalists. At this moment, can you speak for social justice and those at the bottom rungs of society? Our current communications network and media exclude poor people. Simply following so-called impartiality actually will be unfair to some groups.

For news practitioners, truth and discernment are the basis of conscience. But can we maintain our conscience? Interest groups offer benefits—money, advantages, promotion, fortune. The poor and weak only give you sincerity and emotion. Why bother? Nowadays, young journalists face tremendous pressure as soon as they start working. They have to pay the rent or mortgage, utilities, cell phone; technology is changing and the workplace is in flux; and every day they must think about making money.

Journalism is fragile. And journalists have fragile psyches. Honor and professional spirit have declined. You are not that important as an individual. You are doomed to drown in the vast sea of information. In the past, we used to look down on street reporters and paparazzi. In fact, we already are verging on that. Our stable and eternal verities are being challenged. There's a kind of postmodern breakdown in journalism. The breadth of information sources and the speed of transmission are growing; but the traditional gravity of news has eroded. In the past, journalism was conducted in a solemn and righteous manner. Now much news turns into absurd comedy. Take our page today about graffiti on the Great Wall. Ostensibly, we wanted to show that damaging cultural relics is a universal problem. But readers find it damn amusing!

A few days ago, our paper reported about two AIDS patients from Shanxi Province who'd come to Beijing for help. A hospital arranged for free stays, national leaders came to visit, and China Central TV broadcast them shaking hands with the patients. The next day the two guys got phone calls from their hometown, saying you have created trouble and humiliated us; now everyone knows you have AIDS. Their families were thrown into disarray; the son of one patient is missing, the wife of the other ran away. The journalism we used to consider noble has disintegrated.

Chinese media cannot escape the trend; even large news organizations are wild about tabloid news—chickens with four legs or cows giving birth to five-headed calves. But it extends to the most serious things. We still have thirty million Chinese living below subsistence level, and on a traditional holiday we get a vulgar report about a leader giving you a bag of wheat flour and a ten-yuan bill—and spending a thousand yuan for someone to take a picture of him shaking hands with you. What are the real living conditions of the poor on this special occasion? What is their current situation? You can't see it.

I think the biggest threats come from commercialization and the indifference of society. Any political change will have a brief impact, but when the storm subsides, the invasion of commercialism and the disappearance of idealism will cause the greatest changes. Media work needs ideals. Maybe thirty years from now, after I retire, I'll see the media mature and make the transition from political party, interest group, and corporate to truly public. But over the next ten years, the encroachment of commercialism and worldliness will loom much larger than the democratization we imagine.

I would tell young journalists to be brave enough to go against the tide. When everyone else is relying on the Internet, you should not; when nobody's walking, you should walk; when few people are reading profound books, you should read. Put another way, rather than seeking a plusher life, you should pursue some hardship. Eat simple food. When everyone's going for quick results, pursue things of lasting value. Don't follow the crowd; go in the opposite direction. If others are fast, be slow. If you spend an hour walking to work, you'll see and feel a lot more than another guy does on a ten-minute car ride. You might run into a businessman who drives a BMW or Mercedes, or encounter a vagrant, or a fallen tree blocking your way. Such experiences are very important for young journalists.

I tell younger reporters in my department to use as little instant messaging as possible. It may be real-time communication, but it wastes time. Reading good books is better journalism training than computer chit-chat with broken sentences larded with symbols and full of mistakes. Have reverence for the classics, and learn from them—their language, their thinking, their theoretical outlook and methods of analysis.

The greatest reward of journalism is the feeling of participating in society. You can delve deep, come to understand, record what you find, and let yourself be heard. This profession gives you an avenue to contact society and transmit your voice. If you are responsible, you can convey your views and your views may influence others.

Had I followed the usual path to become a public functionary, I might have attendants holding my bags. One of my former schoolmates has such a position. He always speaks cautiously and dares to say nothing; and if he's meeting with a foreigner he goes into a tizzy. Here I am, talking to you. I also hold a notebook, and I'm also recording your questions. You might be a scholar or a president, and we can still talk like this.

II

INTO THE FRAY

Li Yang
李 扬

China Newsweek
中 国 新 闻 周 刊

$\mathcal{L}$i Yang is a bit of an anachronism—a young reporter cutting her teeth in the market economy, but with high ideals and a zest for investigative reporting of the sort more commonly found among journalists a decade older. As an energetic novice with few credentials, she got into reporting simply by trying it, and proving she could do it, when an entry-level job provided the opportunity. Her baptism came at the Beijing bureau of Xinhua News Agency, where she got a taste of the pitfalls of aggressive reporting and came to appreciate the loyalty of experienced colleagues who rallied to her side. Her most important mentor there was Wang Jun, another of our interviewees, who referred us to her. She has left Xinhua for the bigger canvas of a weekly publication, *China Newsweek*—no relation to the U.S.-based magazine, but rather a domestic commercial venture of China News Service, a government news agency established in 1952 to supply Hong Kong, Macao, Taiwan, and "overseas Chinese" media with mainland news and views. Li Yang, now in her mid-thirties, seems to think the cold-bloodedness of the marketplace is the price of opening up new vistas for journalism. Her big news of 2007 was the birth of her son.

I became a journalist by chance; I never had the idea from childhood or anything like that. Both my parents were teachers. My father died early, leaving behind just my mother and me. Our conditions were pretty meager, but we got by. I studied history at Capital Normal University for seven years, four undergraduate and three in graduate studies.

In China—of course the same might be true in other countries—a student of history might not end up doing history. I went to a job fair hoping to find employment with a foreign corporation. It was very crowded, and by happenstance I met the administrator of Xinhua News Agency's "news provision center," actually a kind of sales department, who was there looking to hire a secretary. He asked if I was interested in going to Xinhua. Although I already had an offer from another unit, People's Press, I thought Xinhua was more prestigious, so I went there.

It took a long time before I actually became a journalist. I worked at the news provision center for a year. Then Xinhua underwent some reorganization and my department merged with the information center, where I was an editor for another two years. The job didn't fit my idea of what an editor should do—I thought an editor should be a planner and a rewriter, very senior, and needed reporting experience. Even though I wasn't a genuine journalist, as an editor I had a press card. So I began to look for opportunities to do reporting. I had no connections; I simply started writing stories and trying to get Xinhua to use them. In fact, some were used and picked up by other media.

One piece I wrote, called "Luo Zhewen Decodes Three Historic Misunderstandings," came out of a trip I made with an expert on cultural relics. He told me about some widespread misconceptions concerning China's cultural heritage, including the idea that the Great Wall starts at Shanhaiguan and ends at Jiayuguan. My story was short, but a lot of Xinhua branches ran it. I wasn't even a reporter yet, and I was delighted.

A commentator highlighted my piece in a publication for journalists, and that item caught the attention of Wang Jun, then a reporter at Xinhua's Beijing bureau. Afterwards we became acquainted through reporting about relics from the Three Gorges. He knew I aspired to be a reporter and recommended me to the Beijing branch, where I became a true journalist.

Wang Jun used to tell me mountaineers climb mountains because the mountains are there. Why do we go after news? Because the news is there. Why did I want to become a journalist? I'm not quite sure—my best explanation is that I just wanted to do it, and wanted to do it very much. I was extremely envious of Xinhua reporters who got to meet and interview lots of people and got their stories published. So I started interviewing people as well, and as time passed, sure enough, I became a reporter.

The Beijing bureau had defined beats, and I worked the science and technology beat. My main assignment was covering the city's high-tech area,

Zhongguancun, seventy-five square kilometers with more than two hundred colleges and universities, that was full of vitality but also experiencing problems. In fact, the district was in decline, with many entrepreneurial ventures closing, and I reported on this phenomenon. I also did additional reporting on culture and cultural relics.

I worked at the Beijing bureau for four full years, June 2001 to June 2004. By then I felt it was time to write articles with more depth. As you well know, a news agency transmits stories twenty-four hours a day. We were assessed on the basis of quantity. Every month I wrote several dozen pieces, each very short. The topics were . . . well, to give you an example, things like "Magnolias Blossom at Dajue Temple." For that story I had to get to the place at 8 a.m. and stay until 5 p.m. and describe how the flowers bloomed. This wasn't the existence I envisioned for myself—but it made up 99 percent of my life and was getting more severe, to the point where it could take up 120 percent of my life. This couldn't go on.

China now had market-directed media outfits doing real journalism. I decided to find a job at a weekly that focused on in-depth and investigative stories, incorporating more ideas and viewpoints. My initial hope was to work for *Southern Weekend*, but evidently they didn't consider me good enough. Of course there might have been other circumstances—for instance, their leadership was replaced often, my application materials might not have been seen, the person who recommended me wasn't in a decisive position, or whatever. After half a year without hearing from them, I went to *China Newsweek* because they were willing to take me.

Another reason I left Xinhua had to do with a harrowing incident I experienced while reporting for the Beijing bureau, concerning *chaiqian*—demolition—in the Chongwen District. Demolition crews were beating up residents who were resisting, and dismantling houses by force, despite government bans on such assaults; and the victims were holding a protest on the spot. I went over, took pictures and tape recordings, then returned to the office and spent an hour writing up a piece for Xinhua's internal reference circular, in which I described the beatings, the protest, the bloodstains, people writing grievance letters in blood, and so on. My reporting prompted inquiries from the central government to the district. The authorities didn't want to see such things happen, but at the local level, due to various interests, the situation got very complex and would take five days and five nights to sort out. Finally, the local officials would have to report to their superiors one of two ways: Either the reporter was lying or they themselves would have to step down. Which do you think they would choose? Right, they would say the reporter was lying. Then they would issue various documents full of frightening Cultural Revolution–style language.

That's what happened. The district officials even issued an "Emergency circular regarding the Xinhua reporter deceiving the central authorities and blustering the district leadership." One day a senior colleague in my office said to me: Li Yang, here is some material the branch leaders would like you to look at, but you can't take notes. Then he said: I am going out for a while and will be back in half an hour. He left paper and pen on the desk—he wanted to help me. Two of my big bosses, deputy directors of Xinhua, showed up at the bureau to put in a word for me. They said, however, that, when the government and journalists are in dispute, the government holds the advantage.

Perhaps ten days after the incident, our branch dispatched an investigation group to look into the case and see whether the reporter had lied. My colleagues were very thorough, going over everything to verify the facts bit by bit. They also went to the homes of beating victims. By then the housing management bureau had summoned a victim for a chat—which one of our experienced reporters immediately knew was an indication that they were trying to buy him off. If the person wanted a three-room apartment, say, they would give him an extra room in exchange for his signed testimony that he hadn't been beaten at all.

For an insignificant person like me, that sort of thing would mean disaster and could end my career. Luckily, my colleague reached the victim on his cell phone and asked him to come back right away to talk, ten minutes would suffice. Sure enough, upon questioning, the man admitted that a deal was in the works. When he was confronted with my photos—pictures he'd asked me to take—and also with the fact that the local hospital had records, he said yes, of course he'd been beaten, and he signed a statement to that effect.

This is a long story and I won't dwell on the details, but I also received threatening phone calls at home. The callers said they had all my personal information. They wouldn't identify themselves; nor did caller i.d. show the source. I was terrified—I felt like my skull was being pricked by pins and needles. I asked them to come out in the open with what they wanted, but all the time I was trembling. I live in an unsavory neighborhood, near a long-distance bus station, and once was mugged there. I subsequently changed my home phone number because my mother, who is seventy, also lives with me.

For more than a month, the sky and earth turned upside-down. The torment was beyond description. This event indeed terrified me, and I still feel the aftereffects. But for friends willing to try everything possible to help me, I could well have been sacrificed.

To tell you the truth, when the propaganda chief of Chongwen District visited our branch and offered cigarettes to the bureau head, I thought I was finished. I felt that these officials were all of the same group. This was another reason I quit Xinhua.

Nothing similar has happened to me since.

At *China Newsweek,* I cover politics and current affairs. The work I'm proudest of was about the great Tangshan earthquake of 1976. What got me interested was a long magazine article written in the Chinese style of *baogao wenxue*—reportage literature—by a Tangshan writer named Zhang Qingzhou, who'd been investigating the earthquake for several years. I thought this was a very important report, but that few people would see it—a lot of Chinese publications don't actually get to many readers. So I proposed a reporting trip to Tangshan to interview the writer and others who'd been involved. I worried about whether my editors would dare approach this landmine, a year ahead of the thirtieth anniversary of the quake. What would my bosses think? Would they give me space? Strangely enough, our editorial office approved my proposal.

I spent a week in Tangshan. The writer was happy to talk to me, and that interview went very well. But I also wanted to talk with people who'd held responsible positions when the earthquake occurred. I ended up interviewing Liu Zhanwu, who'd been head of the city's earthquake bureau at the time and remained in that position afterwards until retirement.

It took several attempts to get this interview, in which Liu expressed his sense of guilt. He was quite depressed, and his wife was suffering from breast cancer, which might not have been a direct result of his troubled conscience but surely was related. Every day I thought about how to approach him. He took my phone calls, but broke several appointments at the last minute. So I went to his apartment building and waited outside. When I'd call up, he'd say he wasn't in Tangshan. I'd ask when he'd be back and where he was and where I should I go to meet him. Finally he told me: I can't talk to you, I don't have to talk to you, I don't want to talk. I said: Let's have a meal together and just get acquainted. He agreed, saying: I have only one precondition—I can't talk about this matter. Actually, how could that be? What else could he talk to me about if not for that matter?

I couldn't turn on my tape recorder or bring out my notebook at the outset—that definitely wouldn't work. So we talked about other things, and I waited for the opportunity. It came when I asked if he'd ever successfully forecast other earthquakes. He said yes, five times. I asked which five, and brought out my notebook and clicked on the recorder. By this point, he was no longer hostile. I recorded his five successful forecasts, which he took as demonstration of my goodwill, and he kept on talking. Neither my recorder nor my pen stopped from that point on. In fact, he really wanted to talk about each and every excruciating detail.

My report saw print in early November 2005. My first article, based on Zhang's reportage on the Tangshan earthquake, was quite long. I also did a sidebar about the period leading up to the quake, including prequake forecasts. Another article presented my interview with Liu in conversational format. It was much shorter, only about a thousand Chinese characters.

Readers reacted immediately, with posts multiplying on Internet bulletin boards. Ordinary people were very angry about the missed warnings, devastation, inadequate relief measures, suppression of information, and years of cover-up. Later on, superiors ordered an end to this *chaozhuo*—media hype; so the discussion stopped.

Some stories are not worth great effort; they deserve only passable effort. Others deserve great effort, even if the effort ends in failure. I feel the Tangshan story was worth all the effort.

The greatest challenge for me is the media's eagerness these days for quick success and instant benefit. The organization's goals don't always coincide with the reporter's objectives.

Sometimes editors can be precipitous and impatient. We're told to go get certain information, and that's it. So one day I told my editors that if you want me to pluck a star from the sky, there are two ways: Either I fall off a skyscraper trying or I draw you a picture of a star. Thus is fake news born.

Self-improvement becomes very difficult in such an environment. A reporter for a weekly must have an ample store of knowledge, which takes time to develop, and wide social connections, which take time to build. We must get to the truth of the facts, which also requires time—if my editors hadn't given me a week in Tangshan, if they had said you must get it done today, I would have failed. But I got the time and was able to hang on and keep trying and finally succeed.

During the Harbin water crisis in January 2005, when a chemical spill upstream in the Songhua River forced the city to shut down its water supply, the magazine sent me to Jilin Province, the origin of the spill. I took a 7:30 a.m. flight from Beijing and got to Changchun about 10 a.m., did some interviews, then took a long-distance bus to Jilin City, arrived at dusk, did more reporting, and had to transmit a story by 10 p.m. Of course, there were reasons for urgency with this particular report. But many stories require time.

I came to my magazine with ideals, but in the end my ideals turn out to be just a contract. Being a journalist is hard. You don't have time to read, to make friends, to practice foreign languages. Your accumulation of learning in all fields is greatly limited. Your work revolves around this or that report. You can't always say no; if you say no three times running, or if you fail three times, then it's time for you to be laid off.

It's still early in the development of China's market-directed media; things are still kind of rough and coarse; what can or cannot be done and what our norms should be have yet to get sorted out. All market-oriented media are facing these problems. Among them, *Southern Weekend* fares relatively well, and *Business and Finance* magazine even better. Why? Because they are more mature. They know the process for producing a good report, and the standards required. If a reporter says he needs one more day, he must have his reasons, and nobody second-guesses him; rather, the editors side with him.

Nonetheless, I love this sort of life and find it quite stimulating. What makes me happiest is having my reports published and read. The more people read and talk about your work, the more they trust you and what you say. Isn't this nice? It affirms my feelings from the very beginning—I just wanted to be a journalist.

Despite the challenges, I am on a spiritual quest. While fulfilling my contract, I strive to do worthwhile work. Someday I'd like to complete one or two or three books. Right now that's impossible; I don't have the time and energy. Meanwhile, *China Newsweek* provides a position where I can express myself, and the magazine supplies the space, and people can buy it at newsstands on the sidewalk and read it.

My main principle for journalism is simple: I want to get infinitesimally close to facts and give expression to them in a brilliant manner. As for differences between journalism and propaganda, that's self-evident. Propaganda is a loudspeaker and definitely will deviate from facts to some extent. All the reporters at *China Newsweek* and the good ones I know at *Southern Weekend* completely share the same understanding. Can we be counted as "real" journalists? I don't know. But for us indeed there is no doubt or need for discussion: The goal is to get close. How close you get depends on time and opportunity. Sometimes you have very little time, just half a day, so you don't get close enough.

We've already entered an era of professionalism in journalism. This is seen in the emergence of a batch of market-directed magazines and newspapers as well as the emergence of professional news reporters and canons of news gathering and news writing. I think these are the most important changes in recent years. And change continues to happen—even if chief editors keep getting replaced!

The actual content of journalistic professionalism comes down to nuts and bolts. A small example might be the difference between writing, "Zhang San hasn't recovered from a fright," and, "Zhang San said that he still hadn't recovered from a fright." The first way of putting it begs the question of how you know he hasn't gotten over the fright. The second tells the reader he said it—it gives you the source of the information. There are unlimited elements like this that journalists are continuously cultivating. I never studied journalism, so I've learned in the process.

Another change is reporters' efforts to discover things through their own eyes. At Xinhua, often some department or agency would summon you and give you a text to work with, and you'd return to the office and revise the draft, making a few changes or taking a different angle. Now reporters want to take initiative and find things out firsthand. So when I read that report on the Tangshan earthquake, I wanted to go learn more.

My first suggestion for young people who aspire to be journalists would be that, if you are truly interested, please join in. If you are interested, that interest can take you a thousand miles. If you are not really interested, you're likely to find it a cruel and unbearable job. I'd also say that how far a journalist can travel depends on a very basic thing—whether or not you have firm values. Impulse and interest cannot substitute for values. And values are not merely words, but a complex system of ideas, a consciousness. Without them, when you're halfway down the road you'll feel you can't go any further.

I don't see myself as having a career; I have a profession. That's how I think about it. I actually have Xinhua to thank for my philosophy of journalism. Market-oriented media don't care about relationships among colleagues or family members, or the impact of work on people's lives, or their eccentricities. Please don't talk about that stuff—just news, just business, nothing remotely related to personal solicitude. But I don't think professionalism in journalism should stifle friendship and sensibility. If you really want to know somebody's story, you must learn about the person, get close to his heart, fuse into his life. I think each individual's existence is the most important thing.

· *8* ·

Liu Jianqiang
刘 鉴 强

Southern Weekend
南 方 周 末

$\mathcal{L}$iu Jianqiang found his métier, investigative reporting, in his thirties; environmental degradation, sex workers, bureaucratic mismanagement, and murder are among the subjects he's covered as a Beijing-based reporter for the popular *Southern Weekend*. Meticulous with facts for publication, he also spins a good yarn; his tale about a murder scoop, correct in the essentials, turns out to be a tad overdramatized (another reporter also was onto the story, and it's likely local rather than central authorities called them off). *Southern Weekly*, an offshoot of Guangzhou's official Communist Party newspaper *Southern Daily*, is known for its reports on sensitive social topics and claims the highest domestic circulation in its category, about 1.3 million copies. Leading editors generally take the brunt of political pressure, and turnover at the top is frequent. Liu himself got a taste of trouble after his thoughts on investigative journalism in China led to a page-one *Wall Street Journal* story in late 2007: Worried his reporter had put the entire paper in political jeopardy, the chief editor fired Liu—but within a few months that editor had been transferred and his replacement welcomed Liu back. Meanwhile, Liu continued to publish under pennames, worked on a book about Tibet, and accepted an offer to spend the 2007–2008 academic year as a visiting scholar at the University of California-Berkeley.

I loved reading as a child—American literature, French literature, British literature, and Russian literature, I liked them all. My essays always got praised. So it was quite natural that I would want to become a writer, or a journalist. I lived in the countryside, and, in my mind, journalists were like authors: Both wrote, both were quite dashing and could influence other people, put their names out there, and get famous. But I didn't think about writing news—I wrote essays and short stories.

My aspiration to become a writer never changed from primary school to college. However, if you can't make a living as an author, you don't have a fallback. I majored in political science at East China Science and Technology University in Shanghai, and, upon graduation in 1992, I felt at a loss. It was a transition period; society wasn't as open as now, the government still assigned jobs, but some graduates were just starting to find their own employment. So who found good jobs? People with family connections and powerful backgrounds—not people like me.

The best I could do was return to my home province, Shandong, to work as a propaganda secretary at a medicinal products company in the city of Qingdao. My responsibilities included writing about company matters, summarizing the year's accomplishments, or describing what we were doing in the campaign to build up "spiritual civilization." After three months, I joined my fiancée in Zibo, where I worked for four years in the personnel department of a bank. That job was easy and paid well; in the 1990s, banks were cash cows. But I had no feeling of achievement.

I pondered several paths. I wasn't in the mood to write short stories; I tried a few but they weren't that successful. In my distress, I would leave my office and go to bookstores to buy books. Buying and reading books was my only pastime. But reading couldn't solve my problems. I thought about graduate school, maybe Chinese literature or comparative literature at Beijing University. But my wife was pregnant and I didn't want to leave my family.

Finally an opportunity arose; the best paper in Shandong, *Qilu Evening News* in Jinan, was hiring reporters. A chance to change my fate had arrived. I applied, passed the exam, and was hired on probation; if I failed to prove myself in a month, I would be let go. I'd never done journalism and wasn't very confident, and the lack of security scared me. I couldn't hold up to the pressure, and went back to the bank after just a few days.

Half a year later, the *Zibo Daily* was hiring. By then I regretted deserting that first break. Here was this new opportunity, and I wouldn't have to leave my wife, who was going to give birth soon. So I got a job at *Zibo Daily*. This was 1997 and I was already twenty-eight years old. Everybody except my wife thought I was crazy. I took a pay cut of 70 percent, and had to return the apartment the bank had assigned me, with no chance of getting such a good one from a newspaper. But life was dull and I needed a change.

As you may know, working for a small Party paper can also be very boring. Every day I would follow the mayor and Party secretary around to activities and meetings, and get them to sign off on articles to be published on the front page. Occasionally I'd interview farmers and workers. Very little creativity. Still, that job was different enough from my bank work to be engrossing. I gained confidence that I could be a journalist, do it well, and enjoy it. This was the right choice.

But I also came to realize that my paper was small-time, not real journalism, after all. The way out was graduate school; I took the exams and got into Qinghua University's journalism program, which opened my eyes and helped me understand what journalism should be. During my studies, I had a chance to spend four months at Hong Kong University, and to attend an environmental conference in the United States. These visits broadened my vistas.

When I got my master's in 2003, I was already thirty-four. I could go on for a doctorate and get a stable job as a professor, or I could look for work in the media, but I didn't know where. Xinhua News Agency? I'd have to start from the very beginning and climb the ladder rung by rung, and anyway I was past their recruitment age limit. A paper like *China Youth News* was too gigantic.

Then I saw a *Southern Weekend* job ad, and my heart was stirred. Would I suit this paper? *Southern Weekend*—part of the Southern Daily Newspaper Group in Guangzhou—is still controlled by the Party, but it's market-oriented, relies on circulation, and derives its profits and influence through the market. Since it's a weekend paper emphasizing investigative reports, I wouldn't have to work night shifts or cover meetings; I could cover important issues right away. And my age wasn't an issue. So I submitted my resume and got an interview in Beijing. A few days later they told me: We want you, get ready to report to work, stationed in Beijing. Out of more than six hundred applicants nationwide, they chose three.

There's a little side story here: Just after getting the job offer, I read on the Internet that *Southern Weekly*'s chief editor had been removed for running a long report on former premier Zhu Rongji, and been replaced by someone from Guangdong Province's propaganda department known for inhibiting the media. This was unprecedented in the twenty-year history of the paper. In the past, superiors might punish the paper for something it published, but it would remain in the hands of insiders. Now they'd sent a news censor to manage the place. Would there be a serious turnabout in the paper's direction? I called the deputy editor right away and told him I was having second thoughts. He told me not to worry, saying: The paper won't change that easily—rather, we hope we can change the new editor. So I went.

★   ★   ★

I'm especially proud of my series on *xiaojie*—young misses, or sex workers—published in July 2004. I'd been to the so-called AIDS village in Henan Province, where many people were infected through selling blood. I'd written about the earliest reports informing the world that AIDS existed in China and that the situation in Henan was serious. I'd also attended a Reuters Foundation training course on AIDS reporting in December 2003 in South Africa. In China, the focus was on selling blood, which was seen as the main culprit. As a matter of fact, sexual transmission and drug use also were major routes. I thought the reporting neglected important dimensions, and that sexual transmission would become the main avenue in China in the future; blood sales could be halted once people knew the dangers, but sex was much harder to stop.

At a meeting at Qinghua University, I met people working for a Sino-British project on AIDS prevention, managed by China's Ministry of Public Health, mainly in Yunnan and Sichuan provinces. It included education for prostitutes, since they were an important link in the spread of AIDS. Sex workers were afraid of doctors and police, so how could the educators earn their trust? Through peer education—they would identify the most respected, eloquent, and trustworthy person among the prostitutes, provide her with training, and hope she would pass on her knowledge.

This sounded like a novel topic, a meaningful way to get at important background issues. The story would help show that AIDS did not just come from blood sales, which people connected to ignorant peasants. AIDS was related to sexual activities that people engage in every day. Second, prostitution in China is a formidable matter that nobody talks about realistically. Media would carry stories about police catching prostitutes and fining their clients, and reporters would even write about using ruses to turn prostitutes over to police. It seemed to me such reporters lacked basic compassion and failed to realize that prostitution is a social problem. The Chinese government's attitude, meanwhile, was contradictory: On the one hand, it wanted to do away with this seamy phenomenon; on the other, it was trying to help prostitutes with things like the Sino-British project.

I knew this story would be hard; I'd have to find a prostitute doing peer education and willing to talk with me. A reporter at Yunnan Radio who hosted a nightly sex education program referred me to a doctor working in this field, who in turn referred me to another doctor working in Kunming, in one of the country's earliest spots for monitoring sexually transmitted diseases. I called her and she said she could put me in touch with prostitutes.

Journalists face a lot of problems, including inside the newsroom itself. Would my editors agree that this was a good story? Once I'd persuaded them this story was well worth reporting, they wondered whether I was the right person to do it. You are a man; is it proper for you to deal with a prostitute? This irritated me, and I said a prostitute would talk to a man more readily than to a woman, and insisted on going.

The doctor in Kunming gave me shocking information: Efforts to suppress prostitution over the past ten years hadn't worked; to the contrary, prostitution had grown rapidly despite severe measures. She estimated that, in that city alone, there were at least eighty thousand prostitutes. Sexually transmitted diseases were widespread, with probably two AIDS patients among every hundred prostitutes. Moreover, most didn't know the importance of using condoms.

Several doctors, both male and female, accompanied me to a teahouse, and a young lady dressed gorgeously in a bright red skirt arrived. She'd been trained as a peer educator. We invited her upstairs, and I started asking questions very quietly, worried the waitresses might overhear. To my surprise, she answered boldly; it turned out that prostitution was considered normal in that area and she didn't feel ashamed about letting people know. However, she didn't have a personal story that could move people. Later that night, she took one of the women doctors and me to a nightclub with private rooms where prostitutes drank tea or wine and sang with customers. There I talked with seven or eight more prostitutes. I'd expected to learn a lot. But it seemed that the more young misses I met, the harder it was to find a story. I asked what they'd do if their customers refused to use condoms, and they said in that case we would just not use them. These interviews were a failure.

The doctors thought of another peer educator for me to interview, an eighteen-year-old girl, but since prostitutes never shared their real names or phone numbers they couldn't contact her. I asked the boss of the nightclub to watch for her, and two days later she surfaced and called me. We met at the gate of Kunming Medical College; to recognize each other, she carried a copy of *Family Doctor* and I held a copy of *Southern Weekend*. I felt the power of this report would depend on authentic communication, and tried to figure out how to talk with her on a personal basis and in great depth. We went to a teahouse but it was crowded and not conducive for talking. So I invited her to my hotel room.

Only after the interview was over did I realize that I'd put myself in jeopardy. Local police are very alert about the media, especially a paper like ours that tends to report negative things in their jurisdictions. If someone had spotted me taking a prostitute to my hotel room, without question I would have been unable to prove my innocence. At the time, I didn't realize how precarious this situation was. I was focusing on my task. If I were to do it again in the future, I would call my editor beforehand.

I thought about the subtleties of the situation as I wondered how to talk with this girl. For a regular interview, it would be fine to sit across from each other in two chairs. But I wanted her to feel comfortable enough to talk freely. I said: There are two beds here; you sit on this one and I'll sit on that one. We each leaned against the headboards so that I wasn't facing her and she didn't have to look at me. I took off my shoes off and put my feet up on the bed. Five minutes later, she did the same and began to talk.

Eighty percent of prostitutes in China come from very poor families, often troubled families. She said her family offered no warmth. Her mother had left their village to work in Kunming, and the girl followed, but her mother didn't want her, so she stayed with friends. One day, a friend who called herself a dance hostess—in fact, she was a prostitute—suggested she dance. So this girl became a dance hostess too. She told me her tale, but talked mainly in euphemisms. She seemed very young and lacking in depth.

By then I'd been in Kunming a week and had yet to find the person who could tell the story in a way that would touch people. Nevertheless, this interview was productive. The main result came at the end, when the girl told me about a woman named Yang Shanshan who was a madam in another city, Baoshan. Ordinarily such a person would take a cut for procuring prostitutes. But this woman was exceptionally nice and never took the cut; rather, she tried to protect her "little sisters" and they looked up to her. She asked them to accept that they should wear condoms and have regular physical checkups and give top priority to safety.

This story sounded fabulous. But Baoshan was several hundred kilometers away and I would have to go by plane, and the girl didn't even know how to contact Yang.

Before going down to Yunnan, I'd phoned the director of the provincial AIDS prevention office, telling him that I was from *Southern Weekend* and was hoping to cover the peer education program. His response was: You cannot report here and we don't like the media. He told me how a dedicated local doctor had helped a China Central TV crew arrange to interview an AIDS patient with the promise that the patient's face would not appear in the broadcast. When CCTV broadcast the piece, it did show his face. The patient had done the interview because he trusted the doctor. After the broadcast, the patient went to the doctor's unit with a knife threatening to kill her, and later took explosives to her home, threatening to blow her and her whole family up. The doctor was forced to transfer to another city.

The AIDS office director told me: You media people are very irresponsible. I said *Southern Weekend* was different, that we paid great attention to professional ethics. He still said no, we only receive official media. I asked what official media meant. He said Party papers, the *People's Daily*, CCTV, etc. I said: Wasn't it CCTV that caused trouble for that doctor? He said: We don't care. Unless higher-ups instruct us to, we won't receive you.

I went to Yunnan anyway, of course—officials often turn us down. I called the AIDS office again, but didn't ask for any officials and got a subordinate. I said I was from *Southern Weekend* and wanted to borrow materials on the Sino-British project and other reports. The fellow who answered said to come right away. I immediately took a taxi there and the young guy lent me a book.

In all sincerity, I praised their work, and asked where things were going best. He said they were doing quite well in Baoshan. I said I'd heard about someone named Yang Shanshan and wanted to meet her. He picked up the phone and called a Baoshan project officer and asked him to arrange an interview. That official said okay, just come. I went straight to the airport and got a flight to Baoshan and found that guy.

It's easy to refuse someone on the phone but hard to do it to someone's face. By that night, the young guy who helped me out had discovered that his own superior had rejected my reporting request. I'd made the right decision in going to the airport immediately. The evening I got there, the project officer took me to meet Yang Shanshan at a club.

Yang was an ordinary-looking young woman. In a private room, we had some beer and melon seeds and talked politely. Suddenly she asked: Teacher Liu, may I bring in some little sisters to drink with you? A bang went off inside my head. I knew this was a kind of sex place, so what did this mean? I wondered if I'd have to go through some test with the young misses. But I didn't think Yang would let them do anything immoderate with a reporter. I also thought about whether I could win her trust if I declined. I had to show that I could identify with their lifestyle. I hesitated only a second before agreeing.

In came three scantily dressed girls of seventeen or eighteen. One sat down next to me and leaned her head on my shoulder and said: Big Brother Liu, let's drink. Another filled a large glass with beer and asked me to drink three glasses in a row. I normally don't drink, but I thought for the sake of the story I should be willing to sacrifice myself. In a short while, several bottles were emptied and I was half drunk. However, they still acted respectful toward me. Later I realized that, even in such a place, a young miss normally would not do anything improper; she got regular pay for drinking with you, and you might give her fifty or one hundred yuan in tips, which would provide a decent income, so why should she have sex with you? When I felt dizzy and left for the bathroom, I overheard Yang telling the others: Teacher Liu is a very genuine man—don't make him drink any more. When I returned, they stopped.

The second and third days, I interviewed Yang Shanshan. She was soft-spoken and sweet. She told me her parents had treated her very badly, and she ended up wandering from place to place and running a bar at age fifteen. She also spent time in Burma, as a card dealer at a casino, and made a lot of money; gamblers who won would tip the dealers thousands or even tens of thousands of yuan. But she began using drugs. Her older and younger brothers also took drugs. I asked her about the scars on her wrists, and she was too embarrassed to tell me at the time, but later on the phone she told me she'd tried to kill herself. Ultimately she kicked her drug habit—it's said those able to kick a drug habit are phenomenal people.

She was very industrious. In Baoshan, she worked as a madam at night and at a cell phone store in the day. In addition to educating her prostitutes, she worked with streetwalkers, the lowest stratum of prostitutes. The highest level worked in the nightclubs, the second tier plied their trade at cabarets, and those on the bottom were the "chickens"—*ji*, the same sound as the word for prostitute—who roamed the streets and made a living at roadside shops. Many were older, in their thirties or forties, and they came from the poorest regions of Yunnan; if they managed to earn one hundred yuan, they'd send sixty home for their husbands to buy fertilizer for their fields and instant noodles for their daughters. Yang dispensed condoms and told them how to protect themselves. As she described their pitiful circumstances, she started to sob. She said: This society is so unjust; if not for poverty, nobody would live like that.

Yang truly had a noble soul. In comparison, she was much better off. A few days ago, I called her and she said her money was all gone—she'd bought a house for her parents and once again was poor.

I wrote the story in three installments. Chapter one was Yang Shanshan's own story. Chapter two told how doctors did successful work in Baoshan, with outstanding people like Yang Shanshan and help from the government and police. Chapter three described the situation in Kunming, where doctors were having a hard time because of insufficient government support and the difficulty of overcoming prostitutes' fears. When I asked, police in Kunming denied closing down brothels where the prostitutes would not cooperate, but I learned of at least one instance in which police arrested prostitutes who didn't let the project workers in.

This reporting took me more than two weeks, at substantial cost to my paper; my travel expenses exceeded ten thousand yuan. I wrote the articles in my hotel room, and they had considerable influence. I feel proud about having reported on a serious problem in China to which nobody else had paid much heed.

Another story I'm proud of never saw print. I learned that the vice governor of Henan Province had hired people to murder and dismember his estranged wife, in June 2005. Such a crime by such a high official was a first in the fifty years since the founding of the People's Republic—there'd been cases involving economic or political crimes, but nothing like this. I knew I was racing against the central propaganda authorities: I'd have to report it before they stifled it. I had the contacts and inside information. If I could get the story out before they issued orders to the media not to report it, I would not be culpable of violating discipline, and people would learn the truth. If I failed to report it, it might never get reported, the trial would be secret, and ordinary people wouldn't know what had happened.

Actually, what I worried most about was not the central propaganda department; China's bureaucracy is very slow, and I was fast. I worried that our chief editor wouldn't agree. From the beginning, my immediate editor didn't believe me. How had I found out, and why was I the only reporter who knew? I gradually convinced him—and also myself—that the news was true.

I felt it was my responsibility to pursue a story of such gravity, despite the possibility that, even if I wrote it, my chief editor would not approve publication or, even if he approved, the propaganda department might punish me. I couldn't ignore it—or I would not deserve to be called a reporter.

I figured I had twenty-four hours. I rushed to the provincial capital, Zhengzhou, checked into a hotel, met with half a dozen people, and made a dozen phone calls, still thinking the editors would never approve publication. A provincial-level official murdering his wife! If Xinhua News Agency hadn't reported it, and the government had not made any announcement, no way they'd let a reporter make it public.

I took care to get the facts correct; getting even a tiny unimportant detail wrong could bring trouble. The next morning, when I finished writing the story and phoned my editor, I urged him to convince the chief editor that in the absence of a censorship directive there shouldn't be any problem. By noon, the chief editor hadn't approved but my editor said he'd keep trying. Finally, the chief agreed to make his decision when he got my final manuscript. At 2 p.m., though, a propaganda directive had arrived forbidding public release of this story and ordering the *Southern Weekend* reporter to return to his station.

The propaganda department had learned about my reporting because I myself let it out. I'd not sought information from the police, who I knew wouldn't tell me anything; but later I'd called to get confirmation, thinking that they wouldn't have time to stop the story. I said I was from *Southern Weekend* and wanted to know when they would make an announcement about the murder case involving the deputy governor. I didn't ask if there *was* such a case, which they'd deny. They said: Oh? Go ask another department. This meant the incident indeed had happened. They also called the propaganda department, which called our newspaper and ordered me withdrawn.

Afterwards the *Henan Daily* published some very short pieces on the case, but further reporting was banned.

Later, there was some debate at our office over my having identified my organization to the police. Could I have claimed to be from *People's Daily*?

Maybe I should have said I was from the central propaganda department itself! Some people say journalists should obtain the facts by whatever means for the sake of ultimate benefit. But deception goes against my principles for conducting myself as a person and as a journalist. I wouldn't want to do it.

This case illustrates my greatest challenge: that when I exert great efforts to find out the truth, I can't always publish it. This is not only due to controls at the highest level. Once you find the facts, you must convince your editors and hope the chief editor won't squelch your report. Even though my story got killed, I'm not angry, because I did my best and proved that I am a good journalist. I keep the report in my file, testimony that I once exposed this affair. Publication would have been best, but, if not, it's enough to have found the truth and displayed my talents.

Being a journalist is fun. It's fun to meet so many people and witness so many things and touch on so many subjects. I can learn in one year what would have taken four to five years at the bank. If I'm going to cover something, I browse through stuff and read books and then get to go find out the truth about the issues. I've been to unusual countries, such as North Korea and Sri Lanka, and in China I've been to Tibet, Manchuria, and the southwest region. I like photography and get to take pictures.

Through reporting, I've made friends with many enterprising and down-to-earth people. The topics we discuss—journalism or the environment or AIDS—have social significance. When we get together, we talk endlessly. I feel like I'm learning every day. Granted, it's great to get praised when you write a good story. It feels really nice when people tell you: Oh, you're Liu Jianqiang? I've seen your stories.

My principles for conducting myself in everyday life are the same as my principles for practicing journalism. The number one ethical principle is honesty. Another is protecting sources. Western journalism tries to minimize use of anonymous sources. But China is different; you may have very important sources, and, if you insist on using their real names, they'll be finished—they may lose their jobs and in the worst case even their lives. You should never expose your sources of information or hurt persons involved in your reporting. Sometimes when we criticize and expose high officials, it has no impact. However, journalism also can be too powerful, and can cause great damage. So I am especially careful in this respect. You might say, if you use anonymous sources, readers won't believe you. So be it. The principle is to protect others.

Chinese reporting standards have risen. In the past, if you merely made some revelations or criticized a hideous phenomenon, people would praise you to the skies. Now you need to produce work of high quality. Journalists are better educated, and more people know about the best of Western journalism, so everybody is learning. Journalists want to dig deeper, into questions of justice, public participation, and the right of expression. Perhaps this is not a change in the notion of journalism *per se*. In news reporting, you only need to find facts. Probably the change is within journalists, who feel compelled to pursue things to the political level. Maybe China's special circumstances have moved media's responsibilities a step forward. Journalists are now addressing issues that used to belong to scholars of society and politics.

The fate of journalists in the future is a big question. Employees of large state organizations will have pensions after retirement. But market-driven media are different. Most reporters for commercial media are young people working on one- to two-year contracts. Those in their thirties are considered senior. People like me, at thirty-six doing investigative reporting, are the oldest. There's no mechanism providing assurance that if you are a very good reporter you can have security in the second half of your life. So where will we go? Wages generally go up with age, which might prompt the boss to kick you out. China has lots of journalism schools, but they only hire people with doctoral degrees to teach. It's a very fossilized system. After working many years as a journalist, you may have social connections that you can use to do other things. But I want to continue in journalism.

Still, I am optimistic about the coming five or ten years. While some aspects of the environment are getting worse with each passing day, one area is constantly improving: professionalism. The furious competition requires the best reporting, and, as your horizons widen, you become more professional.

This is an idealistic profession. You'd better not fix your eyes on money, or you'll be disappointed. But if you have ideals, you'll be happy. Although you'll face many vexations, you'll reap lots of spiritual rewards.

Hu Zhibin
胡 志 斌

Then: The First
竟 报
*Now: Beijing Olympic
Organizing Committee*
北 京 奥 组 委

𝒥t was coincidence that we interviewed Hu Zhibin on the first anniversary of his paper's launching—we talked on December 28, 2005. We found him a delightful, ingenuous young man still trying to make sense of a career he'd entered reluctantly. *The First*, a joint venture of the *Beijing Daily*, the *Beijing Youth News*, and a Shanghai newspaper and broadcasting consortium, and part of a growing competitive mix for newsstand and subway sales, targets young urban readers with emphasis on lifestyle and sports and flashy use of pictures. Its name literally translates as "competition news," an adaptation of an original plan to call itself an Olympics paper; lacking authorization to claim such affiliation, the paper nevertheless pays close attention to preparations for the 2008 Beijing Games. Working in the rough-and-tumble environment of a new commercial startup, Hu Zhibin discovered inner resources he didn't know he had and came to appreciate the intrinsic gratifications of news work, but was not thrilled with the stress, long hours, and tenuous financial rewards. Since we conversed, he's taken a job with the Beijing Olympic Organizing Committee, whose media and communication staff has drawn considerable talent from the ranks of local journalists.

I'm a Beijing native. More specifically, I'm a native of Haidian District. In middle school, I had poor grades in science and math, but some interest in history. As a senior in high school, I spent more than ten thousand yuan for math tutoring, but on the national college entrance exams I still scored only 60-something out of 150, while getting more than 100 in other subjects. My career direction apparently was already determined—I would not go into the sciences.

So although my first choice of major was finance, my poor math doomed that prospect. My second choice was journalism and my third law. When I got into Beijing United University, I tried to switch my second with my third choice but was told that would be impossible. So I was forced to study journalism.

I was ignorant of journalism as a profession. My impression was that when people talked about journalists they meant newspaper journalists, but in fact print journalists can't get famous because people read only the content and care very little about the bylines. The print journalist is no match for the television reporter, who can at least present an image.

As an unwilling student of journalism, I nevertheless had to finish. Like other students, I also studied core subjects such as modern Chinese, classical Chinese, rhetoric, Chinese literature, and so on. My major included news writing, interviewing, and journalism history. In my junior year, Beijing was stricken by SARS, school was suspended, and I was unable to complete the courses in photojournalism and video, so I lack skills in this area—although on the job now I both write and take photos.

My first internship was at Beijing TV, with a program on police and law enforcement. I'd get to work a bit past seven every morning and go out with a videographer. Usually we'd cover one story in the morning and another in the afternoon, return to the station and edit the video, work until midnight, and then go home. The next day, and day after day, we'd repeat the same routine. After one week I fell sick, but didn't dare tell the leadership for fear they would think I was too sickly to be a reporter. The experience taught me what a TV reporter's life would be like. I wasn't suited for it.

After SARS, I had an internship at *Beijing Evening News*, mainly covering higher education. In July 2004, I joined *The First*, which was preparing to launch at the end of the year. My first beat was science and technology, which was good for me; it required precision and the ability to explain things in easily understandable language. I also covered some Olympics stories, and when the reporter who officially covered the preparations was hired away by the organizing committee for the 2008 Beijing Games, I succeeded him. Just as I was adding the Olympic beat to my workload, I was notified that I would have to add still one more beat, city and national development and reform. I'm under severe pressure. That's why I had to reschedule this interview twice—I feel very embarrassed about it.

My father was in the military as a young man and now works at a department store. My mother works for a state telecommunications company. How should I put it? There is a bit of a shadow of the Mao Age over my family. My parents and I are all Communist Party members. They stick to their communist ideals. Just as some people believe in Jesus Christ and others believe in Buddhism, there are some who believe in communism. Fortunately the three of us share the same beliefs in this regard. I joined the Party at nineteen.

I did not expect my parents to think much of my work. When you leave home early in the morning and don't return until late at night, they might think you are just out having fun. They may not understand. But gradually they will come around.

I mainly learned on the job. Actually, being a journalist is not a job or a profession, but a lifestyle. It is beyond man's will. On a regular nine-to-five job, or even a regular night shift job, you can plan your time, with different hours allocated to work, family, and other matters. In journalism everything is intertwined. It's not suitable for people who want a regular schedule.

It was at the television station that I began to figure things out. I was doing a piece about illegal gambling. A bunch of gamblers had been arrested and detained, and we went to interview the gamblers. When we finished and came out of the room, throngs of people, mostly the gamblers' family members and relatives, besieged us, surrounded our car, and began to smash the car windows. A bit dangerous.

I became aware then and there of what the job was about. The core of journalism is being there to tell the facts. What motivates a war journalist who puts himself in the way of hardship and danger? Is it the demands of his boss? The journalist could simply ignore them, with the worst consequence being getting fired. Is it money? If so, the journalist could always give it up because money can't buy life. It's neither. It's a kind of desire to let people know the facts, and a kind of spirit that encourages the journalist to do this.

I myself am very timid. When I was small I didn't dare light firecrackers. I'm afraid of small animals, even a little dog or something like that. But if news breaks out, I charge to the front with my camera—whether it's a fire, a hostage scene, or someone about to commit suicide by jumping off a building. As such a timid person, I don't know why I behave like that.

One day last summer, I got a call on our hotline from a reader whose mother was in poor health. She told me her mother's friends had recommended she go see some kind of quasi-divine guy in a certain military barracks who dispensed what he termed "quantum water," which supposedly expelled poison from the body and cured illness.

Quantum water indeed was a fuzzy concept. This guy purported to produce it by sending out *qigong*—vital energy. It sounded peculiar, so I decided to investigate. His business card claimed he was a very famous Chinese traditional doctor in some association located on such and such a floor in a certain building. When I got there, I discovered the place was inside a military compound and not easily accessible to the public. I ingratiated myself with the guard at the gate, who finally let me in.

The supposed clinic turned out to be a cramped basement. Two men and a woman were there, along with a stream of patients seeking the special water. The master came only on weekends, I was told. The woman asked what my problem was, and I said I wanted the water for my mother. She said only registered patients could buy it; they didn't sell to outsiders. I glanced over their registration ledger and saw more than ten thousand people had signed in, a huge number. The water was supposedly processed in a small inner room and cost forty yuan for a liter bottle. It might have been tap water; I couldn't tell. Plus people had to pay for the clinic visit. I was determined to knock this den out.

My first visit didn't produce anything. I decided to join forces with TV people who could conceal cameras in bags. A friend from my television days and I went on a weekend when the "immortal" master was there. My friend pretended to be a patient. The master sat with eyes closed, mumbling diagnoses as he used a stick with a needle fixed to the tip to trace acupuncture points on some sort of box. Two or three patients preceded us, and his diagnosis was the same for everyone—bad heart, bad kidneys, bad spleen. Obviously he was a swindler.

We registered, bought water, and taped the whole thing with the hidden camera. Since we asked more questions than the typical patient and worried they might become suspicious, we left quickly. I took the water to the Chinese Academy of Sciences for chemical analysis. They found no special ingredients. The so-called master turned out to be a harmless old man who'd been manipulated and forced to memorize those diagnoses; others behind the scene were taking the money. This outfit was listed as a high-tech company with Beijing's special technology district. When my story was published, officials promised to get rid of the operation. Beijing TV also ran the story. I felt that I'd made a small contribution.

When the countdown to the start of the 2008 Olympics reached one thousand days, the city of Beijing hosted an event to unveil the five mascots to the public. The organizing committee was inviting one hundred poor kids from China's far west to attend the ceremony. I flew to Gansu Province a few days before, stepped off the plane in Lanzhou, and interviewed non-stop for two days, talking to more than seventy kids. Officials from the provincial education department had invited me to dinner—perhaps they thought I'd been working too hard—and I was supposed to be there at 6 p.m. I was still interviewing at 4, and when I finished my story in my hotel room it was already 6:30. Just as I was about to leave for the dinner, my editors called from Beijing asking for revisions, so I sat back down to work again. This happened several times. When at last I was available, it was past 9 p.m. It was embarrassing.

Over the next couple of days, I visited several remote mountainous areas, starting with the poverty-stricken county where more than two hundred thousand people of the Dongxiang ethnic minority live. This is one of the driest and most inhospitable areas of China—evaporation exceeds rainfall, and people don't plant trees because the roots would draw off all the moisture. The roads are poor; a trip that would take fifteen minutes in Beijing took an hour. The weather was cold, and the kids had holes in their shoes. After a brief discussion, our group decided to donate one thousand yuan to the county to build a water cistern to catch and store rainwater that otherwise would quickly vanish.

The next day we went to a Tibetan area at high elevation. I had no previous experience at such altitude, and, when we visited a middle school there, I had to rest six times climbing the stairs to the fifth floor. I already felt the discomfort at 3,000 meters. The Tibetans insisted on toasting their visitors in the evening—they didn't drink, since they'd reserved the best grain to make this liquor for distinguished guests, even though they lacked sufficient food grain. The combined effects of the altitude and the liquor really knocked me out—but I still had to work on my stories until 2 a.m. At 6 a.m. the next day, we headed back to Lanzhou, which took nine hours. I worked in the car, writing several thousand words on my laptop, so I'd be able to send my stories off as soon as we got back to the city and Internet access. I got carsick and threw up six times.

But I had no complaints; the newspaper had dispatched me, and it was my duty to do a good job. Like a soldier.

Our paper was the first government-sponsored paper to truly operate as a corporation. It's still under the supervision of the Party and propaganda department, but its operations are market-directed, with no government financial support. It relies totally on selling advertising.

Competition among media is intense, and reporters for market-oriented media are under both material and psychological pressure. If you don't get enough stories, your paper deducts a lot of money from your salary. And you feel terribly foolish and inadequate.

My paper has a rule that every reporter doing hard news must go after five stories a week. If you turn in even one less, or if you work on all five but finish only four, your wages get docked. As our paper publishes only on weekdays, that means averaging one story a day. For story ideas, I browse the Internet, look on the streets, get leads from friends or government news releases or public relations firms—there are many channels.

My department covers current affairs and politics. Timeliness and clarity are required. Another department handles in-depth reporting, and most of their reporters probably have to hand in just one story each month. I'd like to do in-depth reporting, but feel that right now I'm too young and lack the qualifications and experience.

You can see changes in journalism month to month. Competition is growing more and more intense. While competing in the news market, we are also tethered by another dragline; we're a propaganda organization that still has to operate as a mouthpiece of the Party and government. Two days ago, a worker accidentally cut a power cable while digging in a Beijing neighborhood, and more than two thousand households in thirty-eight buildings lost power in freezing cold weather. All the news organizations in the capital quickly sent reporters to the scene. However, the central propaganda department authorized only Xinhua to report this story. Nobody else was allowed to report it.

It is difficult to do anything while being pinned down in this crevice. Virtually every day we have the experience of not being able to report what we think is reportable. Sometimes when you toil and even take risks to produce a piece and the authorities don't let you publish it, you feel both chagrined and angry. At this very moment, another voice is nagging at you: You feel chagrin and anger because you are only an insignificant reporter looking at the issue from your own angle, while your superiors are looking at it from above and know how to handle the overall situation.

In my opinion, Xinhua News Agency is not a news organization. It is a propaganda organization. This is obvious. So in China, especially in Beijing, what is news? Right now it's largely service pieces; you can tell people when to avoid traffic jams. Or hotline news: a car crash on the fourth ring road, or someone jumped off a building, or a fire somewhere. Most everything else, including government policy announcements and things like that, belongs to the category of propaganda. It may or may not be relevant to the masses.

Our paper, as you may have noticed, emphasizes service, novelty, and human interest. If we have to play the role of government mouthpiece, we do it perfunctorily and at the same time we provide information. For instance, if the government announces new grain and oil price adjustments, we'll put the old and new prices side by side so the people can see them clearly. If the government wants us to report on the achievements of the tenth five-year plan, we'll try to point out some of the more interesting aspects, such as how many railways shall be built, how many energy-saving bulbs shall be put in place, and how much the water shall be improved, specific achievements related to the interests of the people.

Government press releases often have back stories that are impossible to dig out through normal channels. The government puts a tight lid on these inside stories. You face this sort of thing every day. Yesterday my newspaper asked me to contact the city's development and reform committee about the progress of an environmentally friendly lighting project entailing replacement of bulbs at elementary schools. The committee won't respond to questions. This is no big deal, but for bigger issues it might be a different matter. Today my paper carries a story about police barriers being set up in front of a big department store. Explosives might have been discovered, but the police won't tell you, and they don't let you cross the lines. Once explosives were discovered at a different department store, and, while everyone was trying to get out, a reporter I know from another paper ran inside and got a scoop. I think most reporters would do the same thing.

When we report on Olympic organizing news, we notice that foreign correspondents, say, from Kyodo or Associated Press, ask very deliberate, thoughtful questions. Although the officials evade their questions, we still admire these reporters from the bottom of our hearts. But we're racing to do four or five stories every day. Simply put, we are not really journalists, we are just *mingong*—migrant laborers, forced to make a living doing piecework. Some of my friends who are office workers earn about the same pay as reporters, but if they work into the evening, they get overtime, while we work sixteen hours a day without due compensation.

I think in the next five to ten years foreign interests will enter the media marketplace and we'll see vicious competition; everybody will be attacking everybody else, nobody will gain a leading position, nobody will be able to set rules, and we'll have a period of chaos. Is this really beneficial to the market? That deserves contemplation. As for how the situation will develop, it really is beyond my imagination. All I know is that a war is brewing.

If you take a tour of our paper or any of the other new market-oriented papers, you'll see that all the reporters are completely immersed in their work and hardly sleep. The editors are also like that. I feel that only this kind of organization can survive in the upcoming war be it with foreign news groups or with domestic ones. The day when newspaper reporters leisurely walked to their offices, browsed the Internet, did a little compiling, and waited for phone invitations to attend news conferences are over.

I am sure that I will continue to go to the frontline of news scenes no matter how perilous. As to whether I will be able to practice my journalistic ideals, I really can't decide by myself. This is because, firstly, I am a Communist Party member, and, secondly, journalism still is the mouthpiece of the Party and government and must fulfill propagandistic requirements. I don't think doing propaganda is necessarily bad; you are serving your country. The United States also does propaganda.

Other work involves a process of tempering step by step. Being a journalist is different. A journalist gets new tasks everyday. Some are probably beyond your capabilities, but you try all the same. Being a journalist is a wonderful job that enables an ordinary person fresh out of school to mature rapidly. Print journalists rarely become famous; readers don't really care who writes the stories. But if you write a good story you can win admiration from reporters at other newspapers. And although ordinary readers might not know who you are, it's very satisfying to overhear people on the subway or bus talking about an article you wrote.

Whether a young person accidentally ends up in journalism school like me or goes to journalism school to realize a childhood dream, whether he admires TV anchors for getting the limelight or war reporters on the battlefield, it doesn't matter. My suggestion is that you first learn what journalism is about—don't simply rely on the title of the major. You may find yourself unhappy with journalism as a mouthpiece or tool. You may find yourself unable to adapt to the lifestyle. You may find out journalism is not actually what you want. Many other jobs can equal or better journalism in terms of material gain or mental satisfaction. A person may come to regret the decision to enter journalism—after getting ground up for one or two years, he'll become fickle, lazy, or lax. If you turn into such a person and then want to change professions, it will be very painful. My advice is to think thrice.

· *10* ·

Zhan Minghui
展 明 辉

Beijing News
新 京 报

$\mathcal{Z}$han Minghui admits to having been a lackluster student of journalism. Paternity rather than intrinsic interest seems to have shaped his choices in study and work: his father is a well-known media scholar and professor in Beijing. Zhan became an enthusiastic convert, however, after graduating from the classroom to a shoeleather-reporting job at one of Beijing's feistiest dailies. He relishes the competition and feels well compensated. His brashness in pursuit of stories and his nonchalance about politics are characteristic of a new breed of energetic young reporter arising from the pressure cooker of China's market economy. *Beijing News,* started in 2003, is a joint venture of Beijing's *Guangming Daily,* a fairly staid intellectual institution, and the entrepreneurial Southern Daily Group based in Guangzhou. In aggressive tabloid style, it goes head to head with the *Beijing Times,* racing to be first to accidents and crime scenes, vying for local exclusives, contending for readership and advertising, and occasionally touching political nerves with stories on protests or corruption. Typically, reprisals for overstepping political bounds fall hardest on editorial leadership, but not necessarily without commotion: In late 2005, before Zhan's arrival, *Beijing News* staff staged a well-publicized sickout to protest the dismissals of top editors.

A few days ago, I was in Huairou on the outskirts of Beijing to cover a wildfire that had burned all the way here from Fengning Country in Hebei Province. When we first got the news, no paper sent reporters. The next day the fire was still burning and the media began to take it seriously. Two reporters from *Beijing Times* got there first. Our reporters and a photographer started out at noon but didn't reach the location of the fire until evening because they didn't know the way—and they saw the *Times* people already on their way back to write their stories. Our people could see the whole mountain was on fire. It was spectacular, but sadly, they didn't have any information or people to interview. It was dark and cold, and they didn't have appropriate supplies. Then the photographer slipped and stumbled and broke his leg. They found a local official who drove the photographer to the hospital.

Another reporter and I were out at a couple of cemeteries in advance of the Qingming Festival, the day for commemorating ancestors, when my office recalled me. A photographer and I drove to the fire with a load of provisions—ramen noodles and bread and beverages, and also computers, communication equipment, an electric charger, and other equipment. We reached the area around 9 or 10 p.m., got the injured photographer from the hospital, and brought him to a farmer's house in a nearby village that the others were using as a base camp.

With the reinforcements, our crew now consisted of three writers, one able photographer and one injured photographer, a driver, and two cars. We did interviews and took pictures. Our editors were going crazy. Our task was to do a full page and not let our main competitor best us. It was close to midnight when we sat down to write our stories, and 2 or 3 a.m. when we finished them; transmitting them was difficult since our cell phones couldn't get a signal in this mountainous area, so we had to take our computers and drive twenty minutes to find a signal. When we went back to the village, all six of us packed ourselves sideways onto a small *kang*—a brick bed. It was cold and the bed wasn't heated and we hadn't brought enough clothes. While lying there, we mapped out our next day's work.

Beijing Times's version in the morning was more thorough and systematic than ours. I later learned that one of their reporters knew the local chief of police, so they'd stayed at his home and gotten his help gathering information. The second day, however, would be different.

The next morning, two helicopters from the 38th Army, which is stationed in Baoding, arrived to help extinguish the fire. Firefighters had dammed up a river to form a small reservoir, and each helicopter with a water tank suspended below could make several dozen trips per day, transferring two tons of water each time. China Mobile had dispatched a transmission vehicle to the area after visiting officials discovered that their cell phones didn't work and they had to use the village's three landline phones.

We'd arranged things like this: First, the driver would take the injured photographer home, and on the way the photographer would take some pictures of the helicopters, which were starting their flights around 6 a.m., while the rest of us went on our separate missions. One writer would drive to Fengning to investigate the cause of the fire—the origin turned out to be an old man smoking or burning corn stalks, with the blaze spread by the wind. Another writer would go up the mountain and view the scene of three thousand soldiers and villagers fighting the fire. I would do interviews at the reservoir and firefighting headquarters.

The farmer we stayed with helped me find an unlicensed taxi, for which I paid fifty yuan for the whole morning. When I saw a helicopter, I told the driver: Follow that copter! He was dumbfounded but drove in that direction, so we reached the reservoir and watched the copter drawing water. A local farmer's market had been cleared for the helipad. I had to take shelter in a privy to keep the gusts from the rotary blades from blowing me away.

Suddenly a copter landed and out came a tall army man in an overcoat. The guy carried a digital camera and had been doing aerial photography. I hurried over to greet him and flattered him to the skies: You are really fearsome! Could I look at your pictures? He showed me some, and I asked if he could give me a few, and told him I'd pay him. He agreed and left his contact info. Then I ducked into a small shop to buy him some cigarettes and water; but when I came out five minutes later he'd already left in a police car, and the copter had taken off.

That night I phoned him and asked if he could send the pictures. At first he said it might not be possible because he was inside a local base. I asked him to find a way, and he said he would see if he could go out in the evening and transmit a batch from an Internet bar in the nearby town. And that's what he did. We used two of his aerial pictures, a quite spectacular one on the front page and another showing the release of water from above.

The next day the *Times* was thoroughly defeated! We ran four pages while they had only one. We devoted one page to the cause of the fire, one page to the firefighting scene, one page to overall description, and one to the copter pilot with pictures. My main contribution was to nail down that pilot and crew and obtain the pictures. We paid the army man eight hundred yuan, not bad for him, and the highest freelance pay we'd ever given. In the future, he will be an important news source for us.

The soldiers finished putting out the fire in two more days and immediately moved on to Shanxi Province to fight more fires. I was commended for this story and got a bonus.

I grew up in Yangzhou, Jiangsu Province. My father is from Nanjing, and spent eight or nine years in the navy, returning to Yangzhou after being demobilized.

He worked at the local daily as deputy director of the advertising department, making a good income. Then he decided he needed further education, so he came to Beijing to take exams and entered the journalism program at Renmin University. I was in fourth or fifth grade.

My father completed his master's and PhD in succession, which took him five years. When he got his master's, my mother didn't want him to continue, considering how old he'd be by the time he finished, so he was going to stop. But his roommate suggested he take the doctoral application exam just for fun, which he did without any preparation. And presto, he got in, so he continued his studies. It was said that he was the first journalism PhD from our province.

I hadn't lived with my father for more than ten years, since he'd worked at the newspaper. I spent my childhood with my mother. She managed a foreign trade department, exporting stuffed animals. She was the family pillar; we relied on her for our livelihood while my father was in school. He got a job teaching college journalism at the China Youth Politics Institute, and I moved to Beijing to live with him when I was in junior high.

The beginning was miserable. When I got off the train at Beijing, I saw lots of cars—nice ones, like Cadillacs; I love cars. But when I entered my father's apartment in the dilapidated building that housed teachers' families, I saw nothing but bare walls and empty floors. There wasn't even a bed! I slept on the floor with my father for a week. The toilet kept overflowing. We complained, to no avail. The next week, when we bought furniture and home appliances, brought more bad luck. The washing machine and the refrigerator were both dead on arrival, and we had to have them replaced. My father was too busy to take care of me. For lunch, I would go to a nearby university cafeteria and order the same things—fish-flavored pork shreds and egg drop soup with tomato, which tasted very good at first but soon made me sick on sight.

After a couple of years, my father was promoted to department chair and became even busier, so my mother resigned from her job and came up to Beijing as I was starting high school. We moved to a bigger apartment, and our living conditions improved. My mother took a part-time job in the school library.

My father recommended that I major in law or medicine in college, but I liked neither. Since I was interested in sports—the NBA, Formula 1 racing, and especially soccer—originally I thought about becoming a sports reporter. I got into the international news program at the Beijing Broadcasting Institute—now called Communication University of China.

I entered BBI in 2001 and lived in the dorm. Among twenty students majoring in international journalism that year, I was the only boy, even though previously the major had always had four or five boys. My big classes with several hundred students from various majors were okay, and I could do home-work with other people in my dorm. But the small classes were quite miserable, especially at first when I didn't know the girl students well. I would sit in the front row, with the three rows behind me all empty, and the girls would sit in row five and beyond. It was especially awful when my concentration lapsed and I couldn't answer the teacher's questions. Had there been another guy beside me, he might have been able to give me a hint or something.

As a student, I really didn't know what journalism was or what journal-ists did. To tell the truth, I basically had fun at college; I didn't study much. The atmosphere really wasn't conducive to study. The school has all kinds of specialties, from lighting to digital editing to recording—just about any special-ization media might need. Its reputation trumps everything; of all the anchors broadcasting in Chinese at China Central TV, who is not from this school? My teacher in my very first class, who is now a school vice president, listed students who had passed through there and are now famous anchors and hosts. Indeed, the school has produced many strong graduates. But new graduates nowadays don't get good jobs. I didn't get very systematic training in journalism at col-lege, and aside from writing about European soccer matches for some websites, I never learned anything about sports reporting. So if I wanted to become a reporter, I had to start from scratch.

Beijing News was hiring around the time of my graduation. My father thought it was a good paper, so after an interview with the director—just a two-minute chat—I got an internship. It was as easy as that. It was because the top guys at the paper all knew my father and thought that, with some train-ing, I would be fine. I started my internship in May and got my diploma at the end of June, when they had to decide whether to keep me on. By then I'd been running around for two months and wanted to stay. It was touch and go. One deputy director thought I was frivolous and didn't suit journalism work, but he was about to retire. The director, who wanted to keep me, told me to wait a bit. That deputy director left, and I signed my contract with the paper on July 26, 2005.

My beat is breaking news—we call it "hotline news," which means I go wherever incidents occur. I'm on call Wednesday and Thursday and also for the night shift Monday, but otherwise my schedule is not fixed, and I can take time off when I like. We divide Beijing into three sectors, and when I'm on duty I keep watch in sector A on the west side, because I went to college there and like the area.

Our newspaper has "insider sources"—meaning sources in the police. Dealing with insider information is eerie. The source will send a short text message saying what happened somewhere. Only our director can contact the insider back, and only by text message.

One afternoon in October, I was given an insider news lead about dozens of sheep being killed overnight in the north part of Haidian District. The address we got was correct, but the spot was very hard to find. By taxi, I searched every corner of two villages, checking everybody's sheep and finding nothing amiss. At 8 p.m. I still hadn't found the place and was at the end of my wits. So I walked along the road asking people if they'd seen any police cars. Finally I found the place—a tree nursery on the road between the two villages where the owner kept about forty sheep in a pen. The manager was very cooperative, and I finished interviewing and photographing and got back to the office at 10:30 p.m. and wrote up the story within an hour and a half. It ran half a page under the headline "Unidentified Animal Kills more than 30 Sheep." Our director praised me for this story, and I felt I'd made the right decision in staying with the paper.

Once I had the trust of the leaders, I got better and better at covering my beat. I began to get more assignments and sometimes have five or six at a time.

Our department has more female than male reporters, but for safety reasons the males get sent on night assignments or murder cases, and I enjoy covering murders. The first murder case I covered was thrilling. The victim was the mother of the chief of a police station. Her neighbor chopped her to death in front of her own home. I was the first to reach the spot and the victim was still on the ground bleeding. Throngs of police were everywhere. My task was to interview family members or eyewitnesses. At first I felt uneasy. The woman was already dead and her relatives were crying their guts out; how could I approach them in their distress? Even senior reporters have to overcome this psychological handicap.

In addition to breaking news and crime, I sometimes cover current affairs and politics. On my most psychologically jarring day, I was at the state guest house at Diaoyutai in the morning to cover a visit from U.S. Assistant Secretary of State Christopher Hill, and I could watch TV and use the Internet and eat cake; that night I was breathing dust and combing every inch of a remote building site to investigate the death of a construction worker.

Every reporter must fulfill a monthly quota—on top of our base pay of 1,500 yuan per month, we must complete 2,500 yuan worth of stories, calculated according to quantity as well as quality, with the grading determined by our director. The editors jokingly call me one of our paper's three *jingang*—a reference to Buddha warrior guards—since three of us write the most stories, about forty a month, sometimes more. I'm quite satisfied with my income; for a new graduate like me, monthly earnings of 7,000 to 8,000 yuan are good enough. I don't have to pay for transportation—I get 2,000 to 3,000 yuan reimbursement a month for taxis and rarely take public transport anymore.

I still live with my parents. I want to move out, but my mother won't agree, although my father takes a hands-off attitude.

I see my dad only a few times a week, and we seldom discuss journalism unless I have something specific to ask him. He does mainly theoretical study, so he can give me general coaching, but in practice I have to rely on myself and learn through experience. My schedule conflicts with his: I rise at noon and stay up late. I'm a night owl who can get up in the middle of night to handle emergency news. When I get home, my father has gone to bed, and when I open my eyes next day he is already gone. We rarely see each other, and the only exception is when we watch soccer together. We both like Arsenal, and he likes Milan and I like Juventud.

A couple of days ago, a colleague asked me what a journalist could do if he quit journalism, and then answered himself: Nothing! A journalist is eclectic; he doesn't know everything about anything, but must know something about everything. Knowledge is the basis of everything. I don't like to read, so I don't know much. My dad loves reading—I feel dizzy at the sight of all the books in his study, which used to be my bedroom but the books crowded me out. My greatest challenge is gaining knowledge, since you never know what kind of people and what sorts of things you'll run into the next day.

For instance, today I was covering a story about *chaiqian*—demolition—concerning two brothers whose houses are to be knocked down for a new housing development. The compensation offered is 550,000 yuan but they want 8 million. Of the forty-two households in the neighborhood, forty homes already are demolished, leaving only the two brothers and family members who take turns standing guard. The scene is all shambles and ruins. I brought back a heap of background materials—policies of the township and construction committee and so on.

Experience is especially important in interviewing. I often work with a senior reporter who looks like a policeman and covers a lot of murder cases. This month we wrote about an old man and his grandson who were chopped to death over a fifty-yuan dispute. It is always easier to interview relatives of victims, who are more willing to talk, and much harder to get the suspect's family to talk. And police are least cooperative of all. Suppose a murder occurs in the precinct where I live. When we go to the local police, they may say that, yes, they are handling the case but cannot disclose anything. Or they may say they've passed the case up to the district level. Only after the case is solved might they issue a press release to you. By then the case has lost its timeliness.

So we can't rely on official news sources to get the real story. We try all kinds of means to pry open their mouths. Not that I want to deceive, but we have to use deception. Say we are covering a residential protest, with people blocking roads or picketing about some lack of services. The other side might not want to talk with us, so we'd call identifying ourselves as residents of the area to try to get information. We adopt the same technique with the police. Suppose there is a homicide case, we might pretend to be a family member or relative of the parties involved to try to obtain information. Once we got a tip about an abandoned newborn, but people at the agency taking care of the baby wouldn't tell us anything, so a senior journalist called the precinct police and said his kid was missing, and then had me talk and pretend to be the kid's brother.

Our paper has no rules about representing ourselves except one: we can't masquerade as police. If you do and get found out, you'll be in deep trouble. Once I did pretend to be a cop, to try to get information about a U.S. businessman who fell to his death from a utility pole. The U.S. Embassy and police had sent people and cordoned off the site and wouldn't talk to us. I called the witness who had reported seeing the man fall and he immediately detected something wrong with me so I hung up hurriedly. I was so afraid of trouble coming my way I couldn't write anything.

When a foreigner dies in Beijing, I sometimes have a chance to use my English. A man in the shoe business from Azerbaijan owed money to a Chinese; the creditor chased him and he fell off a building. A French guy with relationship troubles took sleeping pills and jumped off a building. An Italian couple died in a fire. An American consultant dropped dead in an elevator. A cut-up corpse was found behind the Iranian embassy. A Pakistani student at Beijing University fell off the history department building to his death.

The basic principle for journalism is to respect objective facts. You should try to be evenhanded and let both sides involved speak up. If someone doesn't want to talk, that's his problem, but you must ask him. Afterwards, you should have multiple sources for cross-checking.

Once I made a bad mistake covering a car accident. Who was to blame and how did it happen? I interviewed Driver A, and got his story. I tried to interview Driver B, but he was in the hospital and unavailable. It was already 11 p.m. I took Driver A's line, which proved to be wrong—a traffic control guy called later and told us what really happened. That story was a total failure. Fortunately the other driver didn't complain. This experience was a lesson. You must talk to as many people as possible, and the more people you ask, the more you approach the facts.

I despise propaganda—empty slogans like the "eight honors and eight shames." When my former classmates want my help transmitting such things, I tell them to fuck off. Of course, it's necessary to publish some of those things, an appropriate volume of them. At least in an environment like China's. Some formalities must be followed. Our paper does carry Xinhua dispatches on some major matters. But playing the role of the Party's mouthpiece is the job of our superiors. We don't care about them.

I do think newspapers should provide some guidance, but they need to avoid that kind of official tone. If something is a good thing, just describe it the way it is.

There's also the commercial kind of propaganda—entertainment events, where they hand out "red envelopes" hoping to get favorable mention. When I was asked to cover a Shenzhen TV contest, I just wrote it as straight news—the event, the rules, and so forth. That's it. To be used as a hired gun is repulsive to me.

Sometimes people try to bribe us; housing developers offered one of my colleagues three thousand yuan. When we run into such things, we accept the money and turn it over to our office. As long as we hand it in, things are fine. Anything beyond that is not our concern. Then if we have to report on him, we still do it. Our boss can take care of the rest.

Now I know so much more than when I'd just graduated—four years of college can't compare to eight months' work! I most like getting scoops or nailing down issues that nobody else can. Next, I like producing lovely or influential stuff. And a sense of success. For now, these are the things.

I've been a reporter for only eight months. I started out here at the bottom of the trough—I almost wasn't hired. Now I'm doing well. I'll do my beat for a couple of years and see what lies ahead. An editor in charge of in-depth reporting asked me if I might want to do that, and I said forget it; with my current abilities, I don't think I'm capable. Maybe later I'll switch to in-depth reporting, which tempers a reporter but is very difficult—they leave you alone and then you have to rely on yourself. I still think about being a sports reporter. I'm sure it would be quite different than what I used to imagine. I should improve my foreign language ability so that I can be a foreign correspondent. That would be more challenging.

Over the lunar new year holiday, I was on duty at my paper's international department. Several accidents occurred in Egypt. First, a Chinese tourist bus overturned. A few days later, an Egyptian passenger ferry sank, killing more than a thousand people. During those few days, I contacted sources online and interviewed them. We relied mainly on Xinhua reporters and the ambassador and the embassy spokesman. I called Egypt every day. It was cool. I think being on the spot would have been even cooler.

III

IN THE NICHES

Lu Yi
鲁 伊

Sanlian Life Weekly
三 连 生 活 周 刊

*L*u Yi fell into science journalism by happenstance. She's a staff writer for what is probably China's best known newsweekly, a hybrid of politics and current events, culture and lifestyle, with a circulation of 200,000. The magazine's parent company, the Sanlian Book Publication Group, traces its history to the distinguished Sanlian Bookstore and an associated publishing house founded in the 1930s in Shanghai; *sanlian*, meaning "tri-union," refers to three magazines from those days, titled *Life*, *Reading*, and *New Knowledge*. All suspended publication after the founding of the People's Republic of China in 1949, but the company was revived in the 1970s and, after some false starts, a successor magazine was started in 1995. *Sanlian Life Weekly*, also called *Lifeweek* in English translation, has earned a reputation as one of the more serious and responsible publications finding success in the marketplace. The magazine periodically goes out on a limb, and did so frequently in 2006 with a series of cover stories on politically touchy subjects, including one marking the fortieth anniversary of the start of the Cultural Revolution. Lu Yi's specialty earned her a Knight Science Fellowship at the Massachusetts Institute of Technology for the 2006–2007 academic year.

On November 27, 2001—I remember this date very clearly because it changed my life—I got to the building that housed *Sanlian Life Weekly*. The executive editor, whom I'd never met, came down from the twenty-seventh floor and invited me to lunch. While we ate in the dining hall on the ground floor, he asked me questions about what I hoped to do and my thoughts on current international news. Then he asked: Are you done eating? I said yes. He said: In that case, you can go upstairs to get a job assignment.

Later I learned why they'd hired me so swiftly. A science reporter had just left with her diplomat husband for France, leaving a vacancy. And the magazine was trying to meet its weekly deadline the next day. I arrived at the opportune time and was immediately put to work on a science column headed "Good News, Bad News." I sorted five items into two good, two bad, and sent them for layout and printing. No internship or training. This is how I became a science reporter.

Lu Yi is my pen name. My real name is Luo Yanning. But few people know me by that name. I turned thirty in November 2006.

My father, who was from Sichuan Province, went into the army in Heilongjiang Province at age seventeen, and stayed on with the Army Construction Corps, as a bodyguard for the chief of staff. He met my mother there. I'm their only child. I grew up in a small city, Jiamusi, where I had a mediocre education. Maybe due to a bit of luck, on top of my own efforts, I got into Beijing University—Beida—to study law. This was a big deal for our high school because it hadn't produced a single college student for years.

I was at Beida from 1995 to 1999. During that time, my parents moved to Harbin. My father worked for the wasteland reclamation bureau and my mother retired. She'd worked at an electric motor factory, and later a research institute, and was once a very successful career woman, some kind of manager—I remember that in the mid-1980s her salary was more than seven hundred yuan a month, quite impressive at the time when most people made about two hundred. Still, my family is ordinary. My mother had a high school education plus some part-time study; my father got a college education through part-time studies.

I majored in law because my high school teachers pointed me there, but I discovered I also liked logic, advanced math, computer programming, and other science subjects, as well as history. I took extra courses and didn't pay too much attention to my core courses, although I still intended to go into law. In my junior year, I thought about going to the United States to study, and even took the LSAT and got a good score. The problem was tuition. My senior year, I did internships at a district court in Beijing and at several law firms, and began to feel there was something weird about the field. I was idealistic, and thought working in law would promote justice and that everything should be orderly and well regulated. But people who'd earned law degrees abroad were abandoning principles and doing things for the sake of money.

I was among the first batch of college graduates who did not find employment right out of school—I became what we call a *beipiao*, a Beijing drifter. It was an experimental time when you had a choice—you could let your school find work for you, with no assurance of where you'd end up, or you could go off on your own and the school wouldn't intervene, but you gave up the guarantee of a high-status "cadre" job. Probably because I was young, I didn't think this was anything terrible.

Since going off to college, I'd never relied on my parents financially. Beida's tuition was still low, seven hundred yuan, and the dormitory cost four hundred. I did tutoring and writing and other part-time jobs, and was proud of being able to pay my own bills. Upon graduation, although I still wanted to study abroad, I decided to wait and see. I rented my own place to concentrate on English study, hoping to improve my test scores so that I could get a scholarship.

A friend working at a publishing house offered me an easy job translating computer books. In fact, the work actually was for a subsidiary that had bought ISBN numbers to publish foreign works. The pay was fifteen hundred yuan a month, which seemed not bad, as I didn't have any concept about money. I worked at the publishing house for a while, and found the job fairly interesting. I liked this kind of technical stuff.

After nine months there, I job-hopped to the web company Sohu to help run a new science and technology site—whereupon the Internet bubble burst and the plans withered away. I still had a job but it was no longer attractive to me. During this time, I often posted writings to Internet bulletin boards, including that of *Sanlian Life Weekly*. That's where an executive assistant at the magazine, who later became chief editor, read my work. He thought I might be a good fit for science reporting. For a few months, I wrote some stuff for him. That was my introduction to the magazine.

When they hired me despite my lack of experience, I had no idea how to go about doing journalism. But I did like reading science stories, and have a somewhat Westernized writing style that corresponds to the magazine's concept. During college, I'd read a lot, including *Time* and *Newsweek* on the Internet. When I finished assignments, I would spend time browsing for science stories in foreign magazines. Besides *Science* and *Nature*, I found *Scientific American, Discover,* and *New Scientist.*

At that time, we didn't know how to find sources of scientific information firsthand, so our science reporting was mainly translated and edited stuff from abroad. Working this way didn't lead to a sense of accomplishment—plus you would feel a bit guilty. Then one of our reporters wrote an article that was basically a verbatim translation of a *New York Times* story, and the *Times'*s Beijing bureau called us about it, which was a huge embarrassment. Gradually we learned to look up the authors of new scientific papers, find related researchers, establish contacts and interview them. Still, this was not original newsgathering. You were just sitting in the office, sending e-mails and making phone calls. It didn't feel like what a real reporter was supposed to do.

In the spring of 2002, we got news from Associated Press about a major HIV vaccine trial to be held in Thailand. Our magazine had done some reporting on the Henan AIDS crisis and AIDS in Asia, but higher-ups had intervened to keep us from doing any more. We still wanted to give the subject attention, however, so we adopted the roundabout tactic of addressing domestic matters through reporting on Thailand. Furthermore, we considered the human vaccine an important science and public health story. My magazine decided to send me to Thailand.

I was totally at a loss as to where to start. I phoned the UNAIDS office in Bangkok, and the guy who answered, who happened to be a Chinese Thai and could speak a little Chinese, said he could provide assistance once I got there. I got my visa and flew to Bangkok and found that the UN guy really was no help when it came to logistics and details. I visited Xinhua's Bangkok bureau and got no help there either; a senior journalist scolded me, saying that I'd better not report negative things.

Luckily, I had a handbook from the UNAIDS office listing all the NGOs and hospitals working on AIDS in Thailand. I started making phone calls from my hotel room. Most of the NGO people spoke good English. I called them one after another—"fumbling along the vine for the melon"—and finally found a group of vaccine specialists at a university. Through them and a local guide-interpreter I hired, I found a monastery providing free treatment. So I did my interviews there, over about six days.

On my last day, I barged into Thailand's Department of Disease Control without any credentials—we didn't get press cards until several years later. Luckily, they received me. I went from office to office, interviewed the director, and gathered a load of materials—which were all in Thai. When I got back, a Thai teacher at the Beijing Foreign Studies University helped me pick out the most important things.

We published a cover story titled "The AIDS Human Testing Ground" in the spring of 2002 that had strong repercussions. It described the AIDS epidemic in Thailand and the latest methods and research aimed at stopping the spread of the HIV virus there. Our actual purpose was to get people to face the existence of the disease squarely, and to advocate for free treatment, free medication, vaccines, and preventive medicines to control its spread.

This story was probably the greatest challenge of my journalistic career so far. I began to recognize what journalists should attend to. In the course of interviewing people in Thailand, I'd done something very humiliating; since I'd never had professional training, I neglected to write down sources' names. Once I got home and discovered the problem, I had to check back to find out, and the extra long Thai names certainly made it more difficult. As a novice, I didn't note details like time and place either. At this point I began to realize my deficiencies and started paying attention.

I especially like stories about scientific fieldwork. I'm now writing a story from a recent visit to Inner Mongolia about a joint project of the Inner Mongolia Archeology Research Institute, the National Museum, and the State Survey Bureau. This was mainly an aerial survey project, photographing sections of an ancient site from small aircraft, in order to draw up a protection plan. The site occupies a large area and excavation is extremely difficult because many things are unreachable. The desert terrain is hard to cross, and our vehicles often got trapped in sand. No large-scale excavation has been done in recent years, but tomb robbing is a serious problem and protecting the site isn't easy.

I found out about this project serendipitously, from a researcher I met en route to Greece for a conference on European wind farms. The aerial survey aimed at both a clear overall view and discovery of sites not easily viewed from the ground. For instance, paths of canals and streets can be seen more clearly from above. The survey was about half done when I visited. I went as a photographer as well as a reporter. I'd begun studying photography because good pictures of scientists working are hard to come by, and our magazine doesn't have the luxury of photographers to send along with writers. We'd often buy pictures from commercial agencies—and often the pictures accompanying our stories about things in China depicted foreigners.

My first attempts at taking my own photos were discouraging. The pictures I brought back from an AIDS conference in 2004 and a reporting trip on the giant panda in 2005 were pretty bad; our chief editor told me that while *National Geographic* will select the best picture from a thousand good ones, you select one less lousy picture from a thousand lousy ones!

So I looked for opportunities to learn from others. I went to Oman with a fairly famous photographer, He Yanguang, who helped me with technique. I met another photographer, Zeng Yan, who among other things covered science, and with his help was able to produce some pictures good enough for use.

My biggest challenge as a reporter for an independent magazine is getting to sources of information. When the State Council Information Office calls a press conference, it doesn't invite us. When we ask state agencies for interviews, typically they'll decline. Regular channels won't work to get an interview at the Ministry of Health; instead, we have to track down the person's phone number and contact him directly. It's depressing, because although we have the ability to do a good job, we get turned down at the outset.

However, it's getting much easier for me to acquire information. Generally speaking, each story I do demonstrates to people in that field that we are a responsible media outlet and our magazine is a quality magazine, so others become willing to share information. But for fields we have not yet touched upon, the first time is very difficult. Trying to get interviews for our first stories on AIDS, avian flu, astronomy, spaceflight, and so on was extremely difficult.

Nongovernmental organizations are much better than government departments, although each case is different. A person may have never heard of our magazine. Our readers are educated people, including a lot of scholars, but our reach still can't compare to big news agencies and television. We face disadvantages as a small organization. What we are proudest of is that once we start covering a field, the door is open and the problems lessen.

I'm very happy in my work. I have a lot of freedom—freedom of the soul, even if I do have to spend time sitting in the office. Small independent media also have advantages; we don't have a lot of obligatory tasks. I don't have to write about things I don't want to write about, or report things I don't wish to report. Our chief editor and executive editor are both solid intellectuals with the best traditions of the literati. Science reporting in China now doesn't attract advertising income and doesn't entertain the masses, but our editors support it, both financially and in terms of attitude. They pay for me to go abroad to attend conferences, approve of my contacting scientists abroad, and encourage me to go on field investigations, which take time and are not very cost-effective. I feel lucky.

I applied for a Knight science journalism fellowship at MIT because I lack both science and journalism background. I'll spend an academic year there, and plan to take courses in public health, history of science, and journalism. The editors are supportive of me studying abroad.

My husband also is a journalist, working for a real estate newspaper. We were college schoolmates; he majored in philosophy and didn't follow up on his major either. We both feel that being in journalism is following our hearts.

A fundamental principle for journalism is truthfulness. Even more important is impartiality. That means evenhandedness. I think a lot of news stories, including science stories, are written with personal biases—a story is either completely positive or completely critical. Neither is proper. The better approach might be to state the facts and let the reader arrive at his own verdict. Reporting should be separated from opinion. You can express opinions through columns. Of course there should also be freedom.

All reporters come up against their own limitations; you cannot possibly understand everything in all fields, especially in science reporting. When you lack sufficient information, others can easily use you. So reporters must stay coolheaded and vigilant, and must constantly expand their scope of knowledge, or at least know the trends and current thinking in the field. Reporters shouldn't take anything for granted.

Journalism in China is becoming increasingly open, and attitudes toward controversial topics are becoming more objective and pragmatic. During the SARS crisis, reporters would interview a government official or scientist and accept whatever he said as the truth. But now in reporting on avian flu, various publications, including our own, provide more complete information and offer their own reflections and judgment. We also have developed means to talk about topics that in the past would be considered too sensitive.

I'm fairly optimistic; I believe people basically have good natures and a common wish for progress. With rising education levels and more contact with others, the environment will continue to improve. I think professional progress in journalism cannot be stopped. A person's knowledge is like a circle, and the bigger the circle's radius, the more seems to lie outside. There's a formidable amount you don't know, so you must incessantly learn.

Yang Jin
央 金

Nationalities Pictorial
民 族 画 报

*C*hinese media coverage of minority ethnic groups is intensely politicized. Authorities wish to portray an image of harmonious coexistence between the Han majority, over 90 percent of the population, and the fifty-five groups identified as minority nationalities. As a photographer, writer, and editor for a national magazine aimed at spreading knowledge and appreciation of minority cultures while promoting state policies, Yang Jin is among the journalists producing alternatives to heavy-handed pronouncements that induce reader fatigue, mindful that the results may be folksy or facile. She seeks to convey both unique aspects of subcultures and hybrids resulting from minorities' interactions with the mainstream, a process she knows personally. Of Tibetan ethnicity, raised in Gansu Province in northwest China, Yang Jin has benefited from educational opportunities extended to promising students from ethnic minorities, including college in Beijing. In our conversation, she emphasized her interest in the rich and colorful aspects of material culture found among minority groups and her efforts to understand minorities on their own terms, while downplaying the inherent sensitivities of the work.

I'm one of four daughters of Tibetan parents. I boarded at Lanzhou Number One Middle School, the best key school in Lanzhou, in a special class for ethnic minority students, and entered Central Nationalities University in Beijing in 1992. Originally I wanted to study economics, since that's what everyone was doing then, but I got interested in photography, and journalism was the only route to learn about photography. The CNU journalism program actually was under the Chinese department, which meant Han language and literature, and some of my classmates later got jobs outside journalism, but my studies made me more interested in the field.

The transformative event for me was a homework assignment to see the World Press Photo exhibition, the first time it was shown in China. The photos used different angles than those we were used to, and we students found them very exciting. My teacher liked my report on the exhibit and praised me in front of the whole class. I was young then and felt greatly encouraged.

When I was a sophomore, guest lecturers who were outstanding professionals from print and broadcast media assigned us to do actual newsgathering work. We covered meetings of the National People's Congress and Chinese People's Political Consultative Conference, the World Women's Conference, and others. The summer before my senior year, I had internships at Guangxi TV and China Central TV, and got experience with both hard news and features. I like television work; it gives you the chance to do your job independently, or in collaboration with the camera person. It has strong appeal and impact, reaches the audience in a timely manner, and produces quick feedback. A magazine is relatively slow, with a much longer cycle.

I graduated around the time direct job assignment for college graduates was being phased out and selection by mutual agreement was being introduced. *Nationality Pictorial* magazine and I chose each other. I joined the staff as a reporter and editor in late July of 1996.

We introduce readers to the culture, history, living conditions, and various aspects of the minorities. China has fifty-six nationalities, the Han people being the majority. Our publication marked its fiftieth anniversary in 2005. When it was launched in 1955, pictorial magazines were just starting up. *People's Pictorial, People's Liberation Army Pictorial,* and *Nationalities Pictorial* formed a backbone at the national level as pictorials in the provinces and localities gradually came into being. At its height, our magazine's circulation reached more than 300,000. Readership is greater in the coastal area than in the interior minority areas. Subscribers include libraries and museums, Han who want to learn about the conditions of minorities, artists who are interested in minority cultures and want to find inspiration from them, and also some foreigners. We do features, which is telling stories, like the U.S. *National Geographic,* although we have not attained that level.

You may think I'm joking, but I'm telling the truth—the greatest challenge I've faced on the job is carrying camera equipment. Just think about it: I am not big and strong. We go to minority areas, far from cities and transportation facilities. It's not like Beijing, where we can easily take taxis. Sometimes the equipment amounts to almost half my own weight. I may have to walk a long distance with the load on my back. I don't bring just one camera, but two and sometimes three, and at least three lenses. I was a journalism major, so I get excited about good story ideas and have a kind of urge to go. But when I think about carrying the equipment, I think: Aiya, my aching back!

Yet walking on mountain roads or following other people around are not the most tiring things; you walk, you stop to take pictures, and when you are done you keep on going, and you can rest along the way. I can manage the high altitude of Tibet and other relatively harsh conditions. My most tiring experiences have been at fashion press conferences! Most of the photographers there are men with arms this thick. The subjects are female models so the men are hugely interested. The sponsor provides a small platform for the photographers. Everyone elbows one another to get the best spots. Usually they have two sessions in a row, so no sooner do you finish one than you have to rush to the next. There's not enough space for a tripod, so I have to hand-hold a camera with a long lens for more than two hours.

I have a picture of such a scene, taken by my husband, an ethnic Mongolian, who's a reporter with China Central TV. He took it because he thought it funny: amidst a dense mass of strong-armed photographers is a small and slender female photographer with a big camera begging for a tiny spot. Yet I still get excited on these occasions; I still want to do the work, these trials by big cameras.

I really have not done a single story I feel totally satisfied with; if I were to single out one accomplishment, it would be the special section I developed, titled "Charms of Adornment," about minority attire.

Adornment is an extraordinarily good subject with rich and voluminous content. As the saying goes: "People living 10 *li* apart don't share the same sky." China's many minorities each have branches and every branch has its special ethnic apparel and adornments. People living 10 *li* apart may not speak the same dialect. People who belong to the same nationality may have different languages and clothing.

I thought up the idea myself, and single-handedly managed the whole thing from beginning to end. The intent was to go behind the facade of minority cultures. Clothing is a form of historic accumulation; each nationality's attire reflects its development and transformation inscribed on the body.

Here's how the idea came about: A reporter went to the Liangshan Mountains to photograph the torch festival and came back with a bunch of pictures.

I liked the minority garments and asked him to bring me all his pictures, and I created a special section that focused on head adornments. Subsequent issues could do the same sort of thing, from head to toe. The section ran from 1997 to 2004, with a gap for a year and a half when I was in poor health. There were thirty-two installments, some grouping smaller ethnic minorities together, so they cover almost all the nationalities.

The section was suspended again last year when I changed job responsibilities, but there's talk about resuming "Charms of Adornment" for all our editions. *Nationalities Pictorial*, in addition to its Han language edition, comes out in five minority languages: Tibetan, Uigur, Kazak, Korean, and Mongolian. Until 2005, the magazine translated the Han edition into those five minority languages almost word for word. To better adapt each language edition to each ethnic group's needs and better reflect the conditions of each group, we decided to redo each edition independently. We started with the Mongolian edition and are planning the same for the Tibetan edition. So I was transferred from the newsgathering and editing department to the minority languages department to take charge of preparations for the new Tibetan edition. The idea is that, since I am Tibetan, I'll communicate better in doing the Tibetan edition. The content still gets translated from Han language but is geared for that audience. I do speak Tibetan and am studying the written language.

Here's an issue focusing on spring festival. That's a Han holiday, but many other minorities also celebrate the lunar new year, although it may be on different dates. The Tibetan new year in fact is also spring festival. Miao and Yao also have their own spring festival. The Shui people celebrate the Duan Festival, equivalent to spring festival. The Yi people celebrate the Mouth Festival for the new year; according to the locals, after a year's hard work, it's time to give the mouth a festival. Here's a picture of a Yi person carrying homebrewed liquor and pork on his back on his way to visit relatives. Minority customs are blended with some of the Han customs and vice versa; for instance, the Han have adopted a lot from the Manchu. The Gejia people, a branch of the Miao who live deep in the mountains of Guizhou, have borrowed the Han custom of hanging spring festival couplets. There's an inevitable cultural blending.

I organized this feature, thirty-two pages in all, shown mostly through pictures. I work with a contributors' network and several websites, so it is relatively easy to get whatever pictures I need. The most important thing is good planning around a clear-cut theme.

Outside influences are reaching even the remotest areas. I once spent a day and a night with a herdsman's family on the grasslands of southern Gansu. They didn't know much about the outside world; the husband had never traveled further than the county seat, and the wife hadn't even been there. She and their two sons were especially curious about my camera and amazed that their pictures could appear in a magazine. The older boy had just started attending a tent school set up for children of nomadic Tibetans. While I took pictures, he chased a soccer ball all over the grass, a yak following him wherever he went. Suddenly he started singing a song in Mandarin, "Mommy is the best in the world." This kid didn't read yet and didn't know the Han language, and he was singing this song at the top of his voice! His parents and I cheered him, and the more we applauded, the louder he sang. Being Tibetan myself, I felt both excited and touched. Although I could talk to him, he was unable to communicate with my Han colleagues, but he was able to sing that song. He also knows it is a song about his mother and through the song he can express his feelings, although he may not fully understand it.

Unlike reporters who cover specific news events, we emphasize humanistic aspects. Journalists who report on minority affairs, in addition to truly reflecting facts and having morals and conscience, must have the capacity for love and compassion. Many people who visit minority areas complain about poor living conditions. You must learn about and understand their lives, and not accuse them of being dirty and backward. You should not use your own taste as a criterion for judging others. What we do is humanistic reporting.

Transportation and information transmission in minority areas have improved a lot, bringing more people to those regions to see actual conditions. There is more reporting about minorities. And people's curiosity about minorities has grown. At the same time, there are many more information channels than before, so in some senses people are less curious. This seems self-contradictory, but it is the case. Some minority areas have become tourist hotspots, and more tourism generates more attention from the media and more reporting on minority affairs. More people are grabbing our rice bowls. In the past, it was just our magazine. Now others report on minorities too, such as *Chinese National Geographic*, *China Humanistic Geography*, *Minorities Survey*, and *Civilization*.

Media have become more specialized, with more categories and variety. Employment opportunities in journalism have grown; if you are clever or original, even if you haven't studied journalism, you can join in. The competition has increased. This stronger competition is forcing us to do our jobs better.

Still, when you've been in this industry awhile, your enthusiasm diminishes and your inertia increases. Young people who have just joined the profession are the most courageous and most creative, so they are the most likely to make achievements. But they may be overcautious because of their lack of experience. I would urge them to be brave and realize their ideas.

Zhang Xuguang
张 旭 光

China Sports News
中 国 体 育 报

*A*s China's state-managed sports system cedes ground to more professional models of training and organization, and the status and rewards of elite
competition steadily rise, Zhang Xuguang makes the case for the enduring
importance of grassroots participatory sports. She covers what the Chinese call
"mass sports," referring to physical education and recreational sports, traditional
emphases of policy in earlier decades. Zhang also reports on Olympics
preparations, a prestige assignment which turns out to have its own frustrations.
Meanwhile, her paper confronts new challenges from the array of specialized
sports media that have arisen over the past decade in tandem with the expansion
and commercialization of sports themselves. Among the older establishments that
once owned the field, *China Sports News* used to be the country's only sports
newspaper; today, alternative outlets abound at national, regional, and local levels.
The official paper of China's central sports administration, it eschews stylishness
in favor of an authoritative tone, and retains certain advantages. Awarded the
right to use the 2008 Beijing Olympics logo for a weekly supplement, the paper
will become a daily Olympics chronicle during the Games.

When I was young, I dreamed of becoming a journalist. Really, I'm not lying! In elementary school, I was enthralled with classical literature; in the fifth or sixth grade, I read the novel *Dream of the Red Chamber* seven or eight times and drew a family tree of the relationships among the characters. Local television heard about it and came to interview me. Looking into the lens of the TV camera, I thought that to work as a journalist would be fun.

I'm from Heilongjiang Province, in the northeast. I grew up in a small, cold, remote place, and my horizons were limited. I envied children who grew up in big cities like Beijing and Shanghai. Later when I went to college, some of my classmates would talk about using computers or playing the piano. I'd never seen those things.

My parents were intellectuals—my mother was a teacher who later worked for the education department, and my father became party secretary of a district in our city. I also have a brother. I don't know why, but from early on, I had the desire to learn. My parents used to turn my light off, saying I couldn't study any more.

Because of my excellent grades in high school, I got a direct recommendation for admission to Jilin University without having to take the national entrance exams. I had a choice among law, history, or literature, and opted for literature, which included the journalism program. After my undergraduate studies, I continued for a master's in mass communication. I wrote my thesis on news and communication in the May Fourth era, China's new cultural movement of the early twentieth century.

Beijing Broadcasting Institute was interested in hiring me to teach. I also had an offer from *China Sports News*. It was pure luck—I happened to be browsing job ads and saw their ad for reporters, so I took and passed the recruitment test. I weighed the two possibilities and decided I preferred practical work on the front lines. As the saying goes, "When water flows in, the ditch is ready." So I became a journalist. That was more than seven years ago.

In school, I'd had internships at *Jilin Daily* and *Jilin Evening News*, doing economics reporting. Our teachers never really let us off the leash; we were led around and received like guests, and had few opportunities to face challenges or embark on tasks independently.

I started at *China Sports News* in July 1998. Our paper is under the State General Administration of Sports, essentially China's national sports ministry. I was assigned to the paper's new Beijing bureau and worked there nearly two years covering a range of subjects—competitive and community sports, the national exercise plan, events hosted by the city of Beijing, league tournaments. The days were packed.

When I started out, I wasn't familiar with sports. I thought soccer was easier; a goal is a goal, and you can learn what offsides is. In basketball, I didn't know about the 24-second rule or holding or what the referee's hand signals meant, and offense and defense switch so fast. At the beginning, the games could be really baffling; I might know someone had scored, but I wouldn't know why a foul was declared.

I knew I wouldn't remember all the rules just from reading, so at first I'd sit next to someone from the soccer or basketball association, or some coaches, and ask questions. I felt that as long as I was modest enough to ask and learn on the court, I'd gradually learn. Within two or three months I knew basic rules, technical and tactical things, for the most popular sports—basketball, volleyball, and soccer. To this day I still don't know much about less common ones, such as softball and baseball.

I'm no longer covering competitive sports; my beat is "mass sport," or participatory sports, which is quite different. Few journalists in China, definitely no more than ten, specialize in this subject; although many cover it occasionally, and there's some reporting on health and diet and things like that, the media emphasis is elite competitive sports.

I'm one of seven reporters in the societal sports news department, whose scope includes community sports, school and youth sports, sports education, and sports technology, science, and research. Personnel and pages for this department used to fluctuate. Gradually we got regular pages, two or three a week, but there wasn't much momentum. The reporting tended to be event-oriented and provided little service to readers. Beginning in 2006, at my instigation, we started a weekly four-page supplement on mass sports and exercise. The government office that promotes grassroots sports nationwide even allocated some funds for this project.

Covering competitive sports gets routine. And you may end up doing the same thing all your life; if you are an expert on ping pong, you will keep covering ping pong, which can deprive you of broader interpersonal communications and space to develop. Covering social aspects of sports widens your horizons and your social contacts. However, not everyone feels that way. When our department expanded from five to seven people and we needed to transfer personnel from competitive sports, some of the younger reporters didn't want to come.

I wasn't that enthusiastic at first either—I thought of mass sports as ordinary Chinese doing fan dancing or elderly people doing shadow boxing. What fun was that? Then on several occasions I accompanied people from the municipal sports bureau to rural counties where farmers were playing on mini-basketball courts built with money from the national sports lottery. The courts were primitive, with just a backboard and basket, but the farmers said it had changed their life. Previously, they'd followed the sun to till the land and had little recreation beyond drinking and playing cards. With this small measure, they felt the government had helped them solve a huge problem.

Common people need more of this, to feel the fun of exercise and improve their health.

Mass sports are everywhere, as long as you search and observe carefully. If you walk around Tiantan Park near our paper in the morning, you discover that everyone has a favorite way to exercise. Some methods are striking, and make you think: Boy, this is great and should be popularized! Once I saw a lady in her sixties kicking a shuttlecock. She said she could do over a hundred variations. Simply watching her was a great enjoyment.

A story that provides something practical and beneficial doesn't have to be of great significance; it might be quite routine and plain. One of my stories came out of a conference to honor hundred-year-old senior citizens. Usually such meetings are nothing special, but I followed up and visited these old men and women in their homes to observe what might be behind their longevity, from their food and clothing to their cheerful mood, from their shadow boxing to their finger calisthenics.

For another story, I checked out a reader's letter about a neighborhood sports ground being encroached upon; local authorities wanted to pull down public exercise equipment to make room for some other projects. I called the writer of the letter and got more details, and also called the municipal sports bureau, which had procured the area and installed the facilities with public funds from the sports lottery but didn't actually have jurisdiction over the place. I went numerous times to interview the locals, who said it was their only exercise spot and that seniors and children needed it. In fact, officials were obligated to provide a similar area for sports before dismantling the old one for other uses. Our paper ran several stories, and the exercise ground survived.

We've also investigated the reduction of physical education classes and lack of sports grounds in elementary and middle schools. China's main emphasis now is on quality education. The situation is better in big cities, but in smaller ones and in the countryside, lack of facilities can be very serious. Last month, a truck driver who fell asleep from fatigue went off a road in Qingyuan County, Shanxi Province, killing twenty-one students from a middle school who were out there doing morning exercises. They didn't have any sports ground.

I immediately wrote an article on the need to address the issue of school sports grounds. State regulations require schools to provide them, according to enrollment and other criteria. But few schools meet the requirements—not more than half nationwide at best. I publicized good methods for addressing the problem. Some schools trade or share sports grounds. A school in Beijing uses nearby Taoranting Park for phys ed classes. Although the accident itself was horrific, I thought it was most important to figure out what really can be done, unlike the Ministry of Education's response, which was to ban morning exercises from roads! Without exercise, how can students maintain their physical conditioning? Which, according to the data, is quite bad!

I also do Beijing Olympics coverage. I've been covering preparations for the 2008 Games since the selection of Beijing as host city in July 2001. The night of the announcement, I was at the New Century Altar waiting for the last word from Samaranch. Covering the Olympics is not easy; the subject is tied up with government and the volume of information released is not great. Relatively speaking, the press conferences are getting more liberal and supplying information in a timelier manner, but it's what we call "dry goods," mainly in the form of government reports. It takes more work to dig things out.

My newspaper also has an innate disadvantage in aspects other than sports. The Olympic Games are not just a sports meeting; they involve politics, economics, transportation, weather, game venues, etc. Xinhua News Agency has people covering different fields who can produce comprehensive reports with concerted effort. We lack sources in these other fields. The 2008 Olympics are set to open on August 8, and when I wanted to know the possible impact of the weather at that time of the year, I had to make several dozen calls. People who don't know you don't feel at ease with you, so you have to seek approvals and send an outline to be passed from one hand to another and then another; first they tell you to consult the national weather bureau, then they say it should be the Beijing weather bureau, then some research institute, and so on and so forth.

Olympics coverage and mass sports overlap somewhat. The three major concepts for the Beijing Olympics are environmentalism, high technology, and humanism. The idea of a humanistic Olympics is somewhat abstract, but in my understanding it means an Olympics with a harmonious atmosphere. This dimension encompasses game ceremonies and cultural events, as well as the character of Beijing's citizens. The nationwide exercise programs can help raise the caliber of the citizenry and deepen the popular understanding of sports.

I feel the greatest challenge in my work is insufficient command of English. In the past when I went on assignments abroad, I was able to get by in English, and didn't feel it was a problem. But now lots of foreigners, including experts and scholars, are coming to China. People who were involved in the Sydney and Athens Olympics have been here to offer advice for Beijing, and recently a bunch of reporters from foreign news organizations came to share their experiences. I wasn't an English major and can't do a perfect job when I have to communicate face to face or try to follow presentations on very technical matters.

When there were very few sports publications, and few sports pages in newspapers, and papers were much smaller, our paper had a great advantage. Now competition in sports journalism is severe. Newspapers have expanded to dozens and sometimes even more than a hundred pages, with sports news as major content. And many more specialized sports papers exist. Ours is a general paper, covering various fields of sports. So I think the threat is mutual. Our continuing advantage lies in our comprehensive reporting.

The difference between news and propaganda doesn't really apply to sports. Propaganda's objective is to get people to accept certain notions, but sports must make facts speak for themselves. If you don't have a good record, nobody will want to use you for propaganda. We emphasize news and service. But there's a touch of propaganda. Our paper must report various activities and meetings involving sports administration leaders, which smacks of propaganda. But the proportion is small.

The most important change since I entered journalism is that people dare to speak out more. When I began my career, you could feel the restrictions. Grapevine news or Internet items rarely made it into regular media. In sports, fake matches and corrupt referees existed but nobody exposed them; the soccer association was a government department, and nobody dared point to some soccer official and accuse him of wrongdoing. In recent years, media have become more open. The commercial metro papers carry criticism of the government, stories reflecting readers' interests, and hotline news. Sports media report scandals. Wrong is wrong, whether or not they admit it. There is some supervision via public opinion. Limits and problems still exist, but in general things are getting better.

Truth is the first principle of journalism. We often hear stories about fake news, and, as sports news has moved into the category of entertainment, some sports reporting has come under question. In any kind of journalism, truthfulness should be number one. Another principle is depth. You cannot just float on the surface; you must unearth firsthand stuff.

Young journalists should ask a lot of questions, write a lot, and run around a lot. The most important precondition for being a journalist is to be good at communicating. A good communicator can gain a lot from conversations and associations with subjects. Nobody knows everything, so it just won't work if you don't ask questions. Writing requires practice. Only when you have written a lot and can write smoothly will you feel unobstructed. Merely coping with your assignments won't work. At press conferences, as soon as you sit down a complete news release and even its electronic version will be stuffed into your hands. Lazy reporters just copy it down, which can't produce real stories.

When you write stories, it's best to avoid routine and clichés. Some novices simply browse through back issues and see how veteran sports reporters wrote things. In my view, you should have your own ideas. You can browse and learn, but different subjects require different angles. Without your own ideas and questions, you are simply wasting your time.

Ma Yin
马 寅

Titan News
体 坛 周 报

*W*ith the compact stature of a gymnast and the exuberant style of a born storyteller, Ma Yin entered sports journalism as an informed and adoring fan, just as teams and athletes she covered were gaining celebrity. Her knowledge and determination, in conjunction with serendipitous encounters and assignments, made for a career that parallels the steady rise of China's sports industries and sports media. She writes for one of the great successes of Chinese sports journalism, *Titan News*, which began in 1988 as an obscure weekly paper based in Changsha, capital of Hunan Province, and built a national following through scoops and inside information. In 2001, the paper itself made headlines by luring a top reporter away from a soccer newspaper, and paying her royally, to obtain exclusive coverage of the Yugoslav coach known in China as Milu, who would take the Chinese men's soccer team into World Cup qualification for the first time. *Titan* literally means "sports altar," but offers a nifty homonym for the English word, derived from Greek mythology, suggesting size and strength. Still registered and nominally based in Changsha, the paper moved its main operations to Beijing in 2005, the year its self-reported circulation reached 1.6 million. Ma Yin has covered soccer, gymnastics, and diving, and expects to follow the Chinese women's volleyball team through the 2008 Olympics.

In early 1989, I wrote a letter to former U.S. President Reagan. I'd always liked him. I'd read three biographies about him when I was young, and listened to tapes of his speeches, and even memorized some. He started as an actor and became a president. He had the charisma of a statesman. He was handsome, too. After he left office I could no longer see him on TV, so I wrote him a letter. It was a simple letter. The president's office wrote me back, and it was a simple letter, too. But this was an important experience in my life. I wrote about it in an essay that I entered in a national middle school essay competition. The topic was students in the 1990s. The judges thought it was unusual and daring for a Chinese girl to write a letter to an American president. My essay won second place.

From then on, I began writing for newspapers and magazines. At first I sent things to publications for high school students, and later to bigger and national ones. I wrote about students, and about young people's lives. By my senior year in high school, I'd already written thousands of words and won additional prizes.

My dream of becoming a journalist goes back to my first year in junior high. The teacher asked students to introduce themselves in two minutes each. I said my dream was to be a sports journalist and authoritative sports commentator. Now at reunions, my classmates tell me, "You took a straight path." It's true. I'm a goal-directed person. I had my goal and was disciplined in my study. My parents never had to push me.

My interest in sports began even earlier, with the 1984 Olympic Games, the first time China participated. I was ten. We had gymnastics champion Li Ning. My mom subscribed to *China Sports* newspaper and *China Sports* magazine for me, and I'd read the paper every day and the magazine every month and knew a lot of stuff—by middle school I was a walking sports encyclopedia. I didn't know how to play Chinese chess, but I knew the names of every chess player and their records. Later through a schoolmate's mother who was a gymnastics coach, we got to interview Li Ning and his teammates and coaches.

I grew up in Beijing's Dongcheng District and went to a key elementary school and a key middle school. Our study environment was good; teachers encouraged the individuality of each student, and we had a lot of extracurricular activities. I was an excellent pupil, and because of that was passed on from junior to senior middle school with the entrance examinations waived. Due to my academic record and writings, I also was admitted to the department of journalism at Renmin University without having to take the national college entrance exams.

My dad is a soccer fan, and I watched games with him during the 1990 World Cup in Italy. I really got to like the Italian soccer team and gathered all kinds of materials about it that I keep to this day. I wrote down the names of the players from TV and bought a soccer magazine each month. My passion for

Italian soccer continued in college—our class was a United Nations of soccer, with fans of different countries.

This was an important period for Chinese sports. I grew up with the Olympics of 1984,1988, and 1992, the World Cups of 1990 and 1994, and the development of sports media—early on there were *Sports* and *New Sports*, and then *Sports Weekly*, *Soccer*, and *China Soccer* in the 1990s. I followed the Italian A soccer league through college, but in China we didn't know the result of the Sunday game until Tuesday—every Tuesday morning after our second class period, a classmate and I rode bikes to the newsstand to buy *China Soccer* and find out.

My father, a high school principal, had been a Chinese language teacher, and gave me great help when I was starting to write. My mother is finance director of China Youth Press. Her job helped me too, since each employee of her publishing house can get a free copy of anything it publishes, so I had a lot of books to read, and magazines like *Youth Digest*, which introduced me to more readings and had a big influence on me. My path growing up was quite smooth.

My parents say I stopped making rapid progress in college. When I got there, I already knew how to write, and only wanted to learn how to write better. The teaching methods at Renmin University were old-fashioned and didn't encourage creativity and independent thinking. For example, news writing always had to be the five Ws and one H and the inverted pyramid. But real life is not so rigid, and not everyone was going to get jobs at Xinhua News Agency writing telegraph-style news. We had forty students in a class, and some didn't even want to be journalists; they'd applied because of the department's fame, or were there because they hadn't been admitted to their first choice of major, such as finance.

I feel I wasted a lot of time in college. I spent most of my time studying English, French, and math—we had to work hard on math, otherwise we wouldn't pass it, unlike journalism history or theory, which only required cramming before exams. If I'd done better in college, I would have achieved more by now. But it wasn't a competitive environment where students are eager to learn. I sometimes regret that I didn't attend a foreign language school and major in Italian. Now I think it's better to major in a foreign language as an undergraduate and then specialize in graduate school. That's what I tell championship athletes who are my friends when they ask for advice on choosing a college major.

After graduation in 1997, I had job offers from Beijing People's Radio and Xinhua, but no certainty that I could do sports news. So I went to *New Sports* magazine, published by the national sports administration. My dad was bothered; he felt that as a graduate of a prestigious school I should go to a prestigious place. But I wanted to be a sports journalist. I think my choice was right. The publication was small, with a staff of fifteen, but had a good reputation. Its circulation ordinarily is 150,000, although it reached 1,000,000 during the 1992 Olympics.

My first interview was with Wang Nan, who'd just won the table tennis championship in Manchester and was considered a possible successor to the famous Deng Yaping. I went to Wang Nan's home in Liaoning Province to interview her and her coach. This was my first reporting trip, and I was not very confident, so I amassed as much information as possible. I spent several days in Shenyang with the team, and her teammates became my friends. Her parents took a bus from their hometown to Shenyang to meet me, and empathized with me as a young gal traveling and working, since their daughter was young, too.

I was really nervous about my article. Before submitting it, I read it to my mom twice. She said it was good, and my editors were satisfied. As a student, I had the habit of reading my parents every article I wrote, and I still do so for long articles. I like their suggestions and they help me cut down on mistakes.

My magazine had contracted with a publishing house to write a children's book series about Chinese athletic stars. The leaders asked me to select and write about a soccer player, so I chose Li Jinyu, who was playing with a Chinese youth team in Brazil. I'd never met him and had to start from scratch. It took me two days to track down his home phone number in Shenyang, and I talked with his mom, who was cooperative. When Li Jinyu was back in Beijing at the end of 1997—a lovely guy, three years younger than me—he told me to go to Shenyang to see his parents, teachers, and coaches. His mom invited his coach Zhang Yin over, and the coach summoned Li Jinyu's pals and teammates to tell Li Jinyu stories.

A year later, the five people who figured in my interviews were stars—the Liaoning Team under coach Zhang Yin joined the A league; and along with Li Jinyu, players Zhao Junzhe, Li Yao, and Wang Liang were all on the national team. Zhang Yin had spent fifteen years training these kids, and now they were on China's top team, and I became the ideal person to interview them. Zhao Junzhe and Li Jinyu became the shiniest stars, and I felt I was famous too. Many media asked me to write about them.

That kid's book about Li Jinyu became an unexpected stepping stone for my career. It was pure coincidence. We got to know each other when none of us was famous. They gave me their home phone numbers—they didn't even have cell phones then. Our relationship is close and natural—we feel like we grew up together. Wang Liang was just eighteen when I met him, wearing a fur hat and a big cotton jacket. I wondered if this kid could play soccer and didn't take him very seriously. Now we are good friends. When no other journalist can get an interview with Zhao Junzhe, I call him and he answers all my questions.

In 1999, Li Jinyu was playing abroad, while the rest of the Liaoning Team was at the top of the game in China. That was my happiest year. I became like a member of the team. I watched every game they played—on TV if I couldn't go to the field. I helped them prepare for games, sending them videotapes of Team Beijing by express mail so they could study their opponent before the match. Liaoning narrowly missed winning the national championship that year; they won thirteen games, tied eight and lost five. Along the way, they won eight games in a row and defeated all the important teams. I began calling them the Little Tigers, and the name caught on across the country. They were so popular that they felt like at home wherever they went. People believed that Team Liaoning would change the fate of China's soccer. I believed it too. I was totally devoted.

Li Jinyu spent a season playing in France. I saw him off at the airport, and we would talk on the phone every night. His first night, he was staying in a small apartment in a small town with trees all around. He lay in bed and saw the shadows of trees on the ceiling. He was scared. He asked me if he should come back to China since he still had enough money to buy a return ticket. I encouraged him to hang on. He asked me to call his parents for him. He couldn't call because he knew he would cry when talking to his mom. We continued talking on the phone every night. I treated him like a younger brother. He didn't speak French, so he felt very lonely in a foreign country. This situation lasted until his mom went to France to look after him.

The next year, 2000, was the saddest year. Liaoning lost five games in a row, and provincial media lobbied Zhang Yin to resign. He did so, and, five days later, an outstanding kid on the team, Qu Leheng, was seriously injured in a car accident. Zhang Yuning was driving, and many people believed he crashed on purpose. Zhang Yuning had been a key player before 1999, and wanted to leave in 2000, but the club wouldn't release him, so he quit playing. Zhang Yin put Qu Leheng in as replacement, and Qu became a star.

I don't know what really happened, but the tragedy confirmed my belief that the team couldn't go on without Zhang Yin as coach. I felt Liaoning media and the club management were ruining the team's future. If this team had been better protected, Chinese soccer wouldn't be in such straits today. But money had changed many things. Zhao Junzhe had told me that, before the players rose to the top league, they didn't have money, but everybody was happy. Later when they played professionally and had money to buy luxury cars and houses, the fraternity disappeared.

When Qu came to Beijing for medical treatment, I tried my best to help him and his family. Qu's parents were getting old. They'd put all their hopes in their son. After the accident, they aged overnight. They didn't have enough money to pay for the treatment. His parents treated me like a family member. I never wrote about what happened between the players, and Qu didn't want to talk about it either because of legal concerns. I wrote how he was facing life bravely and striving to recuperate. He really was. Every time I went to see him, he ended up trying to comfort me. His positive attitude relieved the pressure on me. In the process, my interview subject and I became good friends. He lives in Beijing now, and on holidays I bring him gifts.

Qu's accident and the changes in Team Liaoning left me feeling lost. I didn't know what I was looking for in sports news. Everything I'd believed and thought I could witness disappeared like air bubbles. I even thought of changing careers. Around this time, *New Sports* was merged into the China Sports Newspaper Company and I was transferred to work at *China Sports* newspaper, covering mostly gymnastics and diving. I hit a trough. Everything seemed meaningless. I did my assignments like a robot. I didn't feel passionate any more.

While I didn't see any future in my career, I did get to enjoy happiness outside work; I met my husband-to-be in this period. Until then, Team Liaoning had been my lover.

In October 2001, China finally broke through a barrier and qualified to compete in the 2002 World Cup. I thought the young kids I used to know ought to be key members of the national team. But only one Liaoning player, Li Tie, was on the roster. So while people all over China were rejoicing at the news, I felt so sad that I cried in my boyfriend's arms for a whole night. Zhao Junzhe called me and said he was crying too, thinking he should be on the team, crying with his girlfriend on the streets of Dalian. He called Li Jinyu, who was crying also. We three felt that they two should be part of creating this success, and I should be the one witnessing the success—but we'd all failed. Reality hadn't happened that way.

The only one who succeeded was Li Tie. He's quite a character, and doesn't talk much. He called me to ask if I'd work with him on a book. So if Li Jinyu was the first step in my career, and Team Liaoning was the second, I can say Li Tie was the third. After finishing my reporting at the Ninth National Games for *China Sports*, I went back to Shenyang to gather materials, and spent a month writing a 300,000-character manuscript. The book was published in January 2002. The title is *Iron Burning*—Li's given name *tie* means iron. It came out at the very peak of China's soccer popularity and made a huge splash.

This book played a key role in my next job move, to *Titan Weekly*. The chief editor, Qu Youyuan, actually had called me before, to ask me to write about Zhang Yuning and Qu Leheng and the accident. I told him, "Sorry, I can't do this, it's against my principles." Later, Qu called me again and invited me to work for them. *China Sports* was official and provided job security. *Titan* was a commercial paper and not so secure. My parents cautioned me to think over the offer carefully. But I'd lost passion at *China Sports*, and I decided to go to *Titan*.

Qu predicted that Li Tie would soon be in Europe, and, indeed, after the 2002 World Cup, he went to Britain to play soccer. Qu wanted me to go live in Britain also and report on Li Tie from there. But I didn't want to leave my parents or my boyfriend. There also were some problems in getting a visa. So I forestalled the trip. But Li Tie called me every day and told me stories that I wrote up. At first everything was interesting. As time went on, his life became routine and the excitement disappeared. Li Tie didn't have much to tell me and I didn't have much to write about. I felt bored again.

Because of SARS, all work stopped for awhile and I had a chance to think. *Titan* had started a new magazine, *All Sports*, and I was writing for that publication as well, just hoping I wouldn't have to write about Li Tie anymore.

In June 2003, my paper asked me to interview Zhao Ruirui, a rising star on the national women's volleyball team, and the tallest player at 1.97 meters. This turned out to be another career-changing incident. I didn't know the team was on bad terms with my newspaper. It went back to the 2002 world championships, when the team purposely threw a game so it would face a weaker opponent in the next game. *Titan*'s beat reporter thought this unethical and called on the coach, Chen Zhonghe, to resign. The coach and players didn't like our paper anymore and refused to talk to us. Nobody told me this background, thinking I'd refuse the assignment if I knew.

When I inquired about Zhao Ruirui's phone number, I was told to get permission from Chen Zhonghe. So I called the coach and told him I was from *Titan*, expecting that would impress him. Instead, he was astonished, and declared, "How dare you call me?" I was dumbstruck, until he explained.

I didn't know what to say. I said, "Coach Chen, please do me a favor. The leadership gave me this assignment. I have to fulfill it."

Chen Zhonghe is a kind person. He said okay and asked me to come to practice, where he introduced Zhao Ruirui to me and instructed her to give me her cell phone number. It was pretty funny—like becoming good friends after fighting.

I read all I could about Zhao Ruirui on the Internet. I learned that she likes to paint, so I bought her a painting journal. At first she didn't want to see me; she only agreed to talk to me on the phone. I wrote her a letter expressing friendship and delivered it with the painting book to her building. She called me and thanked me for the gift, saying she could tell I was sincere. Misunderstanding requires time to resolve, but we could try.

I covered the 2003 World Cup volleyball tournament, in which China's women played well. But the better they played, the more pressure I felt. My paper demanded that I get an exclusive interview with the coach at a time when I felt I couldn't ask anything of him. China was expected to win the championship. The day before, when Chen Zhonghe stepped outside to smoke, I approached him to request an interview. Before he could answer, other people around him said no way. I started weeping. Chen tried to comfort me, saying, "Don't cry. Tomorrow we'll see."

The next day China beat Japan to win the championship. Reporters crowded around Chen Zhonghe asking questions. From the edge of the huddle, I heard Chen say he was really thirsty. I left to get him a bottle of water, and, as the other reporters took off to cover the ceremony, I came back and gave him the water. Chen was moved and talked with me for the next half hour.

My paper saw women's volleyball as the next hot topic and wanted me to continue covering it. I thought this preferable to having nothing to write about Li Tie. I visited their training base in Hunan and tried to get to know them and resolve the misunderstanding.

When I was back in Beijing, Zhao Ruirui broke a bone in her right leg. Our newspaper got the information and published it without my knowledge. One week later, my editor asked me to talk to Chen Zhonghe about something else, and, when I phoned him, he said, "Ma Yin, I trusted you so much, and now you've betrayed me again!" He said Xinhua News Agency, China Central TV, and *People's Daily* all had the information but, considering the Olympics were coming up and the pressure the coach was under, had agreed to embargo it. I told the coach it hadn't been me and I really hadn't known. Our relationship had been improving, and now the friendship I'd spent so much time building would be shattered. I cried, and he said, "Okay okay, I believe it wasn't you."

I spent time with Zhao Ruirui as she was recovering, and came to understand more about volleyball and the team. I also learned about the pressures Chen Zhonghe faced. He'd had a difficult life; during the twenty years he'd gone from a player-in-training himself to chief coach of women's volleyball, he'd lost his father, his older brother, and his first wife. He was devoted to the team. Leading up to the 2004 Olympics, when China had lost all but one game, he was under more strain. We talked a lot. He told me a great deal, perhaps because he didn't have anyone else to talk to, and I reported on our conversations in a special section in our paper called "super-conversation."

I got married in May 2004. I told Coach Chen to work hard over the next four years, and I would witness his success—through the next World Volleyball Competition, World Cup, and Olympiad. My husband and I have discussed putting off having a baby. I need time to work. The Chinese women's volleyball team is the fourth step in my career. I covered the team at the 2004 Olympics in Athens, and plan to write a book about them after the 2008 Olympics in Beijing.

After China lost to Cuba in the preliminaries in Athens, Chen told me he couldn't sleep. He worried about the shame if he lost again. I comforted him and told him to believe in himself and he would win. I encouraged him before the next game, and China beat Germany 3-0. Chen said, "Ma Yin, you bring luck." So I said that, from then on, I'd wait for him before each game to wish him good luck. I came to the arena one hour before each game. And I wore the same clothes every day, washing them each night, because I thought those were lucky too. I did this right up to the final. It was a hard game. We experienced the difficulty and the winning together. I recalled my feelings of 1999. I'd finally found my goal again.

I want to be a good listener and friend to those I interview. A reporter shouldn't beg for interviews, nor intrude on people's lives. We must understand people first, and then we can write good articles. Developing, protecting, and sustaining a good relationship with a worthy interviewee requires time. I can sustain this relationship with old friends, but it gets more and more difficult to make new ones. To many athletes, journalists are a headache because they ask meaningless questions and intrude on their lives. Actually athletes and their coaches are easy to talk to. They don't like journalists because they've been burned too many times; something said in confidence becomes public for the sake of "news."

Sports journalism is becoming vulgar and ordinary. There are so many sports journalists now; dozens or hundreds join the field each year. Some are not qualified; they only know how to hold a microphone and ask shallow questions. They don't think. The other day, Feng Kun, the women's volleyball captain, complained to me about a reporter asking her: "Since you are injured, do you still want to play the game?" Feng Kun said: "If I didn't want to play, I already would have retired."

There used to be few women in sports journalism, and they were respected. But now if you say you are a sports journalist, people think you're doing this because you can't do anything else. Young women become sports journalists these days because they admire star athletes—the ratio among sports reporters now is two women for every three men.

A sports journalist should be interested in sports, but not necessarily a fan. I've lost interest in sport for its own sake. Now I care more about how sports operate and how much work athletes put in. I try to look at sports as an expert rather than as a fan. I have passion, but the passion is different from what it was.

In journalism school, my teachers always emphasized objectivity. But journalists are people with feelings; two of them can write up the same event in totally different ways. There is no absolute objectivity. I think the principle is truth. If you respect truth, even people with different views can have the same news elements. I only write what I hear or know; I don't want to guess what my interviewee is thinking. I don't write many critical articles. If I feel there is a problem, I will tell the interviewee directly. There is no critique without understanding. But once I understand, I know what is wrong, and I think about whether to make it public.

Media competition has gotten intense. When I started in journalism, every outlet had a chance to survive and develop as long as it was willing to reform and adapt. After 2000, such chances don't exist. Now passion and ideas are not enough; you must have financial backing, power, and vision. A newspaper like *Titan*, which started small in 1985 and expanded in 1990, could never do that on its own today. Also, now that *Titan* dominates the market, it's even more difficult for others to break in. In 2005, some sports newspapers were closed because of management and market problems, further strengthening *Titan*'s position. Among sports media, *Titan* is readers' number one choice. Its circulation developed from 5,000 to 1,000,000 and more. But its miracle cannot be duplicated today.

When young journalists think about the future, they always say "After 2008"—that's become a deadline, or the moment to do our best. China's sports and media should be at their peak in 2008. As for how we'll face the quiet after the carnival, we don't know. After 2008 I might rest, become an editor, or change my career path. I plan to write a book about women's volleyball regardless of whether the team wins or loses.

My greatest joy is when the team I am covering succeeds—like Liaoning winning eight soccer games in a row in 1999, and the Chinese women's volleyball team at the 2004 Olympics; but, under Chen Zhonghe's influence, I no longer take winning and losing as seriously as I once did. I used to think it was such a pity not to reach your goal after so much hard work. But Chen Zhonghe is stronger than I thought. His maxim is: "Do it well every day." Do what you should, so you'll have no regrets. I've adapted this to mean be happy every day. This is now my attitude towards life.

IV

OVER THE AIR

Liu Qian
刘 茜

China Central Television
中 国 中 央 电 视 台

*C*hina's entry into the television age corresponds with the start of economic reforms and opening up to the outside world in the late 1970s. The former Beijing TV was renamed China Central Television in 1978; for another decade or two, until cable proliferated and provincial and municipal stations began raising programming challenges, CCTV was king, and its influence and resources still are unrivaled. Besides the main channel CCTV-1, whose evening news broadcast remains the country's most-watched regular program, the station now offers fourteen additional channels, including the English-language CCTV-9 and others for sports, culture, music, and movies. Its postmodern new headquarters, designed by the firm of Rem Koolhaas, was built in anticipation of the 2008 Olympics. Liu Qian, a graduate of China's main training ground for broadcast journalists and technicians, reports for the economics channel, CCTV-6. A plum position in terms of status, the job is not cushy; she describes a relentless pace, limited reporting time and airtime, and other pressures and constraints similar to those encountered by her peers in the United States. Although CCTV does have news units known for crusading ideals, Liu Qian's experience suggests how routine itself can come to dominate news work.

I watched China Central Television from childhood, and felt TV was full of mystery and TV anchors conveyed noble feelings. It's different now; the industry is much more developed, and people no longer see it as mysterious.

I'm from Anhui Province. My father works in education and my mother in commerce. They had little influence on my becoming a journalist. In the early 1990s, the journalism profession was admired, and many young people of my generation dreamed of becoming journalists. Going into journalism seemed a natural thing for me. I graduated from Communication University of China—it was called Beijing Broadcasting Institute back then, and most TV anchors were graduates of BBI.

Many of my high school classmates envy me for being a journalist at CCTV. I started working there in 1998, and have been there since, eight or nine years now, doing economics reporting. My beats are real estate and tourism, but I'll do spot news or urgent stories too. I've experienced many things and gotten to know a lot of people. I've witnessed many changes in the economics field. Since 2002, I've also overseen the work of some younger reporters.

A journalist's responsibility is to uphold justice through the power of public opinion—to inform, monitor society, and solve real life problems. Economic news most often is about positive changes, such as the growth of successful enterprises. But problems arise in development, unresolved problems for ordinary people. I want to help solve practical problems. This is my journalistic ideal.

My most memorable reporting experience was helping rural migrant workers get their salaries, back in 2003. A small construction group from Hubei with about seventy or eighty migrant workers hadn't gotten paid for two months. I don't know how they got my phone number, but nevertheless they called me. I went to the site with a crew. It was in Beijing's Haidian District, beyond the fifth ring road, very far away. When I got there, the workers were negotiating with the boss. I think the presence of CCTV intimidated him. When we started interviewing, he became worried, and promised to pay the workers the next day. But the workers worried that, once we left, the boss would break his promise. So I phoned district labor officials. The next day, the workers called me to say they'd gotten their money. They wanted to take me out to dinner. I said it wasn't necessary—that they'd worked hard and needed the money to go back home and celebrate the holidays with their families.

Was this report influential? Other channels did pick it up. But most important is that I helped solve a problem, and helped people who needed help.

The media industry is changing rapidly. The numbers of both print and television outlets have increased greatly since the late 1990s. CCTV now has multiple channels—for news, economics, sports, international; and for big news stories, all the channels send out teams. It's similar in newspapers and magazines. Everyone competes to be first, or to get the best angle or a unique approach. This requires both physical and professional dedication.

The good thing about these changes is that better reporting emerges, with diverse voices and perspectives. This benefits readers and audiences. They get more complete knowledge of events. We're pushed to do a better job. For example, when we cover meetings, we try to report from the perspective of ordinary people's concerns.

The competition can get untidy. When I go to print media and the Internet as sources for news, I find that catchy headlines are often exaggerated. Even major newspapers can be misleading. Some reporters don't take time to understand and make sense of an event. Sometimes media repeat rumors without checking to find out that they didn't actually happen.

New journalists have passion and energy but lack experience and sometimes ignore rules. They need to be thorough. Competition is not the be-all-and-end-all of our profession. We should not compete for news blindly, to the extent of reporting false news. Even though timeliness is important, truth is more important. Truth is the fundamental principle of news. It is the same for journalists around the world. News also must be thorough and objective.

In my view, news and propaganda are consistent and often overlap. They are both based on facts. Propaganda is not telling lies. It is fact-based. There is no false news in CCTV. It is the mouthpiece of the Party and the government. And it is also the mouthpiece of the people.

Journalism is a quick-study profession. You have to read materials and master specialized knowledge in a very short time. I go out reporting every day, sometimes doing three or four pieces in a day. My time is not my own. If there is a major news event, we have to cover it continuously, with no weekends or holidays. I just came back from an international tourism conference in Shanghai, and I'm about to go to Henan. I also have vacation plans in Europe. I have family but no children. My husband is in media also, in management work, but he understands what I am doing.

When you're young, you are strong, energetic, and fearless, like a newborn bull. After so many years, I feel tired and stressed out, and not as strong. Every year new people come in. The competition increases. Being a journalist is a kind of life experience, but the day comes that it wears on you. If an opportunity arises, I might consider changing careers.

· *16* ·

Ai Da
艾 达

Then: Beijing Television
北 京 电 视 台
Now: China Central Television
中 国 中 央 电 视 台

*H*er performance as a student intern at China Central Television earned Ai Da a job reporting on China's archaeological heritage. Protective parents and a solicitous boyfriend thought she was traveling too much; so although she enjoyed the work, she left after a year for the smaller pond of Beijing Television—although within another year she'd returned to the CCTV job she'd liked so much. When we spoke with her, she was still at BTV, in training and not yet assigned a permanent beat. Like rookies everywhere, she seemed willing to take any story tossed her way. BTV, established in 1979 as a municipal station with a single channel, has expanded to thirteen channels; with satellite relays nationwide, it claims to reach an audience of 250 million. Yet in Beijing, it remains overshadowed by the much larger CCTV, earning neither great repute nor particular notoriety until an embarrassing episode in the summer of 2007, when the station aired what turned out to be a phony story. Submitted by a freelancer and ostensibly shot with a hidden camera, the piece purported to document street vendors selling steamed buns filled with chopped-up cardboard. National media, including CCTV, picked it up; ten days later, BTV announced on its own evening news that the report had been faked. The freelancer was arrested, fined, and sentenced to a year in jail for bringing disrepute upon the bun vendors.

My life path looks smooth, but I worked hard for it. My father is a broadcasting administrator in Changchun, capital of Jinlin Province, and, under his influence, I grew up interested in radio and TV. When I was young, I dubbed for radio stations and hosted children's programs for our provincial television station. My mom works at a bank. I'm an only child. It's said only children are spoiled, but that wasn't true for me.

My dream was to be a journalist, so I majored in journalism at Beijing Broadcasting Institute—now Communication University of China. I was chief editor for our college newspaper and did an internship at China National Radio, where I got experience reporting China's two major meetings—the National People's Congress and the Chinese People's Political Consultative Conference. My academic record enabled me to continue for graduate studies at Renmin University without taking entrance exams, and I completed a master's in communication. My thesis was about prospects for digital television in China.

My second year of graduate school, I did a three-month internship at CCTV-2, the economics channel, at a half-hour magazine news program that does long explorative stories. There I got to know the whole process. Later a classmate referred me to the News Center at CCTV-1, and there I became a real journalist, mostly doing short pieces. I'd go out with a cameraman and was responsible for planning, reporting, writing, editing, and transmitting the results. After a year at CCTV, I've just transferred to Beijing TV, doing similar work.

College gave me basic professional training in writing and news judgment so I won't make elementary mistakes. On the job, you can learn nonlinear editing and other technical operations in two weeks. What we learned in college is more important.

I started out with journalistic ideals, but in practice I was likely to exaggerate the facts. For example, in reporting on an auction, I said a bidder had raised a paddle a certain number of times, but actually I didn't count—I guessed. The director said the number was not realistic and asked if I'd counted. I said no. I am still learning.

For CCTV, I often traveled to remote places on archaeology stories. In late 2004, I spent a month reporting on an excavation of imperial tombs from the Western Zhou Dynasty, discovered in a mountain at the edge of a small town in Shaanxi Province. I went to the site daily, and, whenever there was a big discovery, I'd record and write a script and send the report back. Through this experience, I learned that archaeology is not only about finding the treasure; inside the research team are different ideals and views.

I also reported on the discovery of an ancient city gate at Yangzhou, in Jiangsu Province, that enemies supposedly had never been able to breach. It's a big site and difficult to show on camera; it looks like piles of blue bricks, without a clue that it used to be a city gate. I tried to convey its historical significance and need for protection, using computer graphics to help viewers visualize the story. I don't know how the audience responded, but reviewers at the station thought it was good. I think it also had weaknesses—my on-camera explanation was wordy and the editing could have been better.

I took a job at Beijing TV for personal reasons: My boyfriend, a teacher at Beijing Telecommunications University, doesn't want me to travel as much. BTV at first felt very small. CCTV has more advanced technology, and more sources. Things CCTV would never report become news on Beijing TV. On the other hand, many things I did at CCTV had no connection with anybody's daily life. In Beijing, I report on familiar things and small events that are closely connected to people's lives. BTV has hotlines, and we get many tips from the public. I now think the public always knows more than journalists do. I didn't feel this way at CCTV. But at BTV, I experience it everyday.

We have no serious local competition; the Beijing papers don't threaten us, because TV is still people's first media choice. We watch and analyze how CCTV covers some of the same stories, but we can't compete with them, because we don't have as many resources.

I'm still in training and don't have a specific beat; usually they ask me to do what other journalists don't want to do. For example, there's a frozen waterfall in a small town near Beijing. It was a minor story and the place is hard to find. So I went.

During the National Day holiday in October, I reported on extreme pastimes, going to three places to race a car, bungee jump from a cliff, and ride a rollercoaster, and telling the audience what it feels like. No other journalists wanted this assignment, so they gave it to me. The auto racing was the most difficult; I only got my driver's license a year ago and don't drive often. The car was a souped-up Jeep and the ride took a minute. They gave me some safety instructions and said I'd be fine, that I couldn't get injured even if the car turned upside down. The ride felt like being pulled up to the sky and then tossed down to the ground.

I also do some investigative reporting. Recently I did one such report about an online service that claimed to help college graduates check their diplomas. The service was unauthorized, and personal information could get to illegitimate users. During my internship, I went to Tianjin to investigate child labor. Kids of twelve or thirteen would tell you they were eighteen, and even knew which zodiac animal belonged to the year they supposedly were born. We did a report that didn't run, maybe due to pressure from somewhere; but, after I'd left the program, other journalists did broadcast the story. Investigative reporting poses danger for journalists. My parents don't want me to do it.

Reporting is becoming more comprehensive. There's also more emphasis on stories of ordinary people instead of big subjects like industrial or agricultural development. We used to regard news and propaganda as the same. Now we separate them. I think propaganda is a positive thing: It aims to achieve a good purpose through reporting.

The most important principle for news is objectivity, and then immediacy. The journalist should not influence the progress of an incident. Our job is to inform. National interest and social stability also are important.

In doing interviews, ordinarily I introduce myself. Sometimes when it's the only way, we use hidden cameras. But we are very careful to protect people's identities by blocking out faces. We try to focus on the event, not the people in it. We need to respect their rights.

We do live reporting more and more, and it's more complex and difficult than I'd imagined. I didn't realize it involves so many people—reporters, editors, signals, satellites, cable, all backed up to guarantee the signal won't be lost. Live reporting is planned, too, with a script and every step carefully prepared. Sometimes live reports are spontaneous, such as at traffic accidents. But even weather coverage is planned. If the forecast is for heavy rain, the TV station finds out exactly when, gets everything ready, and waits for the rain to fall.

I don't know if live reports in China are just imitations of the Western model. I think it's fine as long as reporters are not just showing off. Putting reporters on camera brings a sense of immediacy, and also helps build the station's brand name.

TV is the most powerful medium. We can see its importance from the spot the television occupies at the center of the home. This is why I want to be a TV journalist, although the work is hard. In TV, you can't base a story on a phone call; you have to go there. When we go out to report, the cameraman carries equipment weighing dozens of pounds, and I carry the heavy tripod. To set up a story, we need to make many calls, but many people don't like to be interviewed. People know they have the right to refuse an interview request, especially when you are doing negative reporting. So I often get rejected. I still travel and am gone for two or three days at a time. When I'm editing, I often work alone in the studio until nearly midnight. My scripts go through many reviews. Sometimes I'll feel good about my work, and it gets trashed. Usually that's because I didn't do a good job.

TV people have a saying: Women get used to working like men, and men get used to working like animals. Many TV journalists look older than their age and are in poor health by middle age. I've seen "60 Minutes." The hosts like Dan Rather are old but experienced, very sharp and analytical. I'd like to still be doing this when I am seventy.

The Chinese TV journalists I respect are unknowns. The public admires the anchors, but anchoring is very different in China from in the West—here the anchors just read the script. I know this, so they don't impress me. I respect journalists who work hard, have good news sense, think deeply, and report from perspectives that don't occur to others. These sorts of journalists are not treated as models, though, so they don't have much influence.

• *17* •

Xiang Fei
向 菲

China National Radio
中 央 广 播 电 台

*X*iang Fei is the nearest to a media celebrity among our interviewees; having spent years as a late-night radio talk show host in south China's Fujian Province and later in Beijing, she gained national fame after counseling a fugitive from murder charges to turn himself in. Subsequently she helped persuade two more fugitives to follow suit. Xiang Fei already had legions of loyal listeners on China National Radio, which calls itself the "voice of China." Founded in December 1940 in the caves of Yenan, the Communist revolutionary base area, the station relocated to Beijing with the founding of the People's Republic in 1949. As television became the dominant delivery mode for news and entertainment, radio branched into diverse formats, with talk shows emerging as staple fare from the 1990s on. Xiang Fei's patience, concentration, and mellifluous enunciation of the standard Mandarin required for broadcast made her a natural for what she regards as an intimate medium with an important educational role. She believes her sunny personality helps her deal with the sometimes harrowing confessions that come her way, and she balances her single-minded intensity at work with an ability to relax off the job. In 2006, Beijing's Newstar Press published her memoir of radio work, *I am Xiang Fei*.

My parents were in the military, and we lived in many places and with people from all over the country. My parents came from Sichuan Province and spoke Sichuan dialect. I spoke Mandarin, the national language, very well. Eventually we moved to Fujian Province, which has many local dialects. When I'd go to buy groceries, vendors often demanded higher prices from me because they thought I was from outside Fujian.

I studied history at Fujian Normal University, expecting to become a teacher. Instead, after graduation I got a job as a reporter at *Fujian Information and Consultation News*, covering science stories. My big problem was that I easily got carsick. I spent most of the time working on stories in rural areas, where transportation is not convenient. I would ride buses and take anti-nausea medicine. Sometimes I'd visit three or four counties in a single day, so I'd have to take three or four pills, which put me to sleep. My luggage got stolen—no big deal, as I didn't own anything valuable. But I'd still be sleeping on the seat at the last stop when everyone else had gotten off the bus. I began to worry about my personal safety and quit after a few months.

I got a public relations job in a big joint venture company—still using words, but I didn't have to travel and was paid 1500 yuan a month, a high salary for the time. I worked there for a couple of years and did well.

Around this time, the mid-1990s, specialized radio channels were emerging for economics, city life, music, and so on, with live broadcasting. It was an era of reform and transition. A friend who knew Fujian Economics Radio was recruiting hosts encouraged me to apply because of my command of Mandarin—now speaking good Mandarin became advantageous. Other friends said that, if I passed the station's test, they would treat me to dinner. Just for that dinner I gave it a try. Of seven hundred people who took the exam, two were selected. I was one.

The leaders in the radio station didn't know that I had no intention of working there. They offered me 600 yuan a month, less than half what I was already earning. They said they understood I got higher pay at the company, but that I'd have high social status as a journalist, since I'd be a government functionary, and that after training my pay would go up according to national standards, although it still wouldn't reach my current level very soon.

I asked what kind of program I'd be hosting. The station director said they thought I would be good for night talk shows—specifically, for hosting a broadcast from 10 p.m. to midnight called "Voice of the Heart at Midnight." I was shocked. This was a famous program in Fujian, with top ratings even against TV. I'd listened, and didn't fathom how people could call in to air private problems with thousands of listeners. Callers to that program had lost loved ones, or were contemplating suicide, or felt confused about their future, or were getting divorced or having extramarital affairs. They wanted the host to help them. I was in my twenties. I didn't have experience with divorce—or even much experience with love. What would I be able to do? The director said I didn't need to be a psychiatrist; I just had to listen, talk to callers, and think about the audience.

What made them think I could handle it? As part of the exam, they'd asked me to tell a story about myself. I talked about my first birthday away from home. I boarded at school. My parents were traveling on business and I didn't expect to see them. But my mom unexpectedly showed up with bananas. At the time, our family was not well off, and bananas were not that easy to buy. We parted at the school gate, and I watched my mother go. I would never forget the sight of her back, the grey day, and the yellow bananas. I was thinking that, when I grew up, I would buy my mom a box of bananas to return her love. The radio people found my story moving and my language vivid and descriptive, suitable for radio.

I decided to try; if it didn't work out, I could go back to the company. For a while, I worked two jobs—the company during the day, the radio station at night. Within a week I realized I loved radio. In the corporate world, I had to deal with bureaucrats—officials in customs, tax, and commerce departments. I had to please those people and say things I didn't want to say. This made me uncomfortable. Actually I hated it. At the radio station, I found I had a simple and equal relationship with colleagues and listeners. I didn't have to please my listeners superficially, and neither did the listeners have to please me.

So I resigned my company job to join the radio station. I had just one month of training instead of the usual three because of the difficulty of finding late-night program hosts. Our schedule is the opposite of normal people's—sleep by day, work by night. And the psychological pressure is huge; everything you deal with is negative, unhappy, angry, and, if you cannot handle this, you'll be crushed. One famous host committed suicide during my time there, and such things have happened elsewhere.

I hosted that program three nights a week from 1996 to 2001. I'd finish work one day, sleep half a day, then prepare for the next day. I didn't have weekends or holidays; on the contrary, those days were my busiest days. Once for the mid-autumn festival, I volunteered to work three consecutive shows so other hosts could go home. From 7 p.m. to 1 a.m. I went without eating, until a guest brought me a mooncake.

I learned a lot. One night, two hours, fifteen calls. When you get a call, you must identify the main points in two or three minutes, and at the same time summarize from the discussion something that might be helpful to other listeners.

The program had varied formats on different days. Monday featured interviews with people in different professions. I interviewed people who do make-up for celebrities, a "spiderman" who cleans skyscrapers, embalmers, nurses from infectious disease hospitals. Tuesday revolved around topics raised by news stories, with live call-in discussion. Another day focused on literature and art, and included interviews with writers about their works. Another offered consultation for psychological problems, with expert guests. Another helped middle school and college students deal with confusions of growing up. Another format was just letting listeners talk.

Sometimes the unexpected occurred. One listener called to tell me he wanted to die. I tried to dissuade him, and called on other listeners to help him. We also called agencies that could intercede with his attempt to kill himself.

Night program hosts don't only take calls and interview guests; we're also journalists, so, when something big happens, we have to cover it. In June 2001, Hurricane Swallow hit, and regular programming was preempted by hurricane coverage. I'd come to work wearing a miniskirt and heels, and was assigned to report from a fish farming area. Some of the fishermen who lived in cabins along the coast were staying out because they were worried about their fish and shrimps. It was very dangerous.

The radio station assigned a male reporter to take care of me; he was a recent college graduate, a very small guy, and I thought I might have to protect *him*. I wanted to exchange shoes with somebody, but no one wanted to wear high heels into the hurricane, so I took off my shoes for the bus ride to the coast. The wind was blowing trees into the street. I began to feel carsick and wanted to throw up, but dared not. When we got to the ocean, others tried to make me stay inside, saying I could convey what they told me to the station by cell phone, but I insisted on going out. The young guy held me around the waist to keep me from blowing away. I wrapped my cell phone in a plastic bag, leaving a hole over the speaker.

In the end the hurricane made a turn and landed a dozen miles from where we were. We went there to report on the post-hurricane situation. On the way back, I threw up in the car, but now my job was done and I didn't have to worry. My shoes were ruined.

The next day the station put out a list to commend reporters who'd done a good job. My name was listed first. I was awarded 200 yuan, with which I bought another pair of shoes.

At the end of 2001, I felt I'd hit a plateau. I wanted to improve, to reach a higher stage. China National Radio needed somebody to do interviews and features. A friend recommended me. In addition, I had a boyfriend in Beijing, and it was harder for him to give up his career to start over in Fujian than for me to go to Beijing. So I transferred to National Radio. Their shows were still prerecorded, and I started hosting a recorded twenty-minute interview show. At the end of 2004, the leaders asked me if I also would take on a live talk show from midnight to 1:30 a.m., since I had experience with such programming.

By this time, I'd been living a normal person's life for three years: I'd married my boyfriend, I went to work and got off at normal times, and could buy groceries and go home and cook dinner. I had weekends and holidays. Life was beautiful. The thought of going back to live studio work again and not getting to bed until 3 or 4 a.m. seemed much harder now. I said I needed to talk to my husband.

I didn't realize it, but my husband knew I wanted to accept the job: He said you are not discussing this with me, you are just notifying me, and if my health allowed he didn't object.

China National Radio has about 150 million listeners all over the country, though not all tuned in at the same time. The highest numbers are for morning news and 10 p.m. to midnight. Our late-night talk program airs five days a week, and I'm responsible for Monday and Thursday. Listeners don't actually call in, but send text messages over cell phones during the live broadcast. In forty to fifty minutes I'll get 1,800 to 2,000 messages, and many more don't get through. The messages arrive on two computers in my studio. There's also a website maintained by listeners.

For a long time, radio programs preached. I use storytelling; it's a more effective way to show what is right and wrong, what is beautiful and silly, what is good. The result is something like radio drama; I play the female roles and find a male host to play the male roles. I also call on listeners to tell their own stories.

On Monday I tell stories of ordinary people; on Thursday I focus on urgent choices in life. I can't talk for ninety minutes straight, and I can't fill the time with music either, since this is not a music program. I wanted to make the program deep and helpful at the same time. I thought about times I had faced hard choices—such as should I give up career for love and marriage? We constantly face choices in life. If we make the right choice, we'll be happy; if it's the wrong choice, we'll be sad. So my program became about teaching how to choose. Listeners can send me messages commenting on different choices in life—to divorce or not, to borrow money or not.

I design and broadcast the entire program—choose the topic, find the music, read and choose the messages, also read news and commercials, all by myself. Once a Japanese TV crew from NHK visited my studio to shoot me doing the show. One person shouldered the camera, one handled audio, and there was a director and a translator—four people. They said in Japan five to six people would be needed to accomplish what I do on my own.

Live talk programs are one-to-one, although the one could be millions of listeners. When I talk to them, I feel I'm talking to an individual. I am each person's friend.

Gu Haijun was a murder suspect on the lam. As a young man in Sichuan, already married with a son, he had accidentally killed another youth after an argument. He adored radio and listened to it day and night. When he watched TV, he didn't feel connected with the anchor. But when he listened to the radio, he felt the host was talking just to him.

Gu had a factory job in the south. He spent 680 yuan—one year's savings—to buy a cell phone. On February 4, 2005, a few days before the spring festival, he sent me a message, saying he was a murderer at large, now at a crossroads of life, and wanted my help. His cell number and the location, in Foshan, Guangdong Province, showed up on my computer. I asked my producer to call that number and provide my cell phone number. But whoever answered said somebody else had sent the message.

That night's program was about a son with a secret he'd never been able to tell his father: When he was seventeen, he'd run away from home after his dad beat him, and gone to another province and become addicted to drugs. His dad found him, apologized, and begged him to return. The son wanted to go back, but not as a drug addict, so he took two months to shake his habit before going home. But now there was a distance between him and his dad—who died suddenly from a brain hemorrhage before the son ever disclosed his problem. The son didn't feel he could tell his mother or sister either. He could only talk to us.

That night I was advising listeners to make choices carefully, to hold on at crucial moments, that a few steps could determine your whole life. At the end of the program, I also thanked Gu Haijun for trusting us enough to want to share his experience.

In fact, Gu regretted sending the message. He couldn't sleep the entire night for fear the police would come and catch him. But nothing happened. The next morning he did call me on my personal cell phone, and we kept in contact for thirteen days, over the spring festival holiday. I had to talk with him secretively because my parents live at my home and I didn't want to worry them.

At first he was very depressed. He was alone at the factory; other workers had gone home for family reunions. He'd committed the crime at nineteen and been a fugitive ever since; he was now thirty-one years old. Having been on the run for so many years, he thought about dying.

I first persuaded him to have the courage to live, and offered some legal advice. He didn't dare consult police or lawyers. He was from the bottom rung of society, not educated. I thought he should turn himself in to the police, but didn't say so directly. Instead, we chatted.

I asked what he'd been doing since his escape. At first he'd worked underground digging coal, and as a porter carrying big bags. He was exploited, earning only three yuan when others got ten, but he couldn't do anything about it. One day a truck ran off the road into a ditch to avoid hitting him. He wanted to help the driver, but dared not, because, if the police showed up, he would be found out.

I asked what good things he'd done. He said catching thieves. I told him he was a good man, and that everyone makes mistakes—he'd been young when he got into that fatal fight. He didn't kill intentionally. He was in a bathhouse and put on someone else's flip-flops, and that person found out and beat him up, so he came back with a knife and stabbed that person on the butt. He cut an artery and that person died; and he hurt someone else after fleeing, so he was wanted for two crimes.

I asked about his hometown. He said it was mountainous, and that he liked mountains and didn't want to labor in big cities. He just wanted to go home and work in the fields and be with his wife and kids. He said he had a son who didn't do well at school. I said a son needed his father. He said he didn't know how to teach his son. He said his mom was in poor health and his dad got drunk and beat his mom. I said if he were home, he could help protect his mom. I made him realize that there were many things in life he couldn't leave. He couldn't just die. His mom, wife, and son needed him.

He said he'd tried to commit suicide several times without success, and that he'd been living a miserable life. For the past six years, he'd go to work at seven in the morning, go to bed at eight in the evening, and then sit awake from midnight until four in the morning, because that's when the police are often active. He couldn't stand it anymore.

I helped him sort through his thoughts and asked him what he wanted to do. If you are not afraid of death, I said, what else are you afraid of? If you were sentenced to death, at least your family would know where you are. If you died as a vagabond, no one would know.

I said I couldn't guarantee he wouldn't get a death sentence, or how many years he'd be sentenced to, but it was possible that if he turned himself in he'd get some leniency.

On the third day of the lunar new year, I was out shopping when he called me and said, Sister Xiang Fei, I've decided to report myself to the police. If I am not afraid of death, what else is there to fear?

I felt relieved. He had made his choice.

His case would be heard and judged back in Sichuan. It didn't matter where he turned himself in, so I suggested he report to the police in Guangdong. He said he dared not. He didn't want to go to Sichuan either.

I said then come to Beijing and I will accompany you.

He didn't tell me when he would arrive. One day I just got a call from him. He was across the street outside the radio station, and didn't dare cross because of the sentries guarding the gate.

He'd never been to Beijing; yet here he was right outside my workplace.

He told me he was dressed in new clothes. I said I was wearing a pink jacket.

It was the ninth day of the lunar new year. Few people were out. It had snowed a little. The sky was grey.

I saw him from the elevator. He had a red suitcase and wore a brown suit. I went to escort him across the street. He saw me and came toward me. I held out my hand and said hello, I am Xiang Fei, are you Mr. Gu? He put out his hand, then withdrew it. I kept my hand out. He rubbed his hand on his suit and shook hands with me.

Over the phone, he hadn't realized our differences. Now he felt it. He felt inferior.

I asked if he was scared, but he said he felt peaceful after seeing me.

I looked at him. He didn't look like a criminal. He was just one of my listeners. Handsome, small, very clean, in his brand new suit. Over a year, he'd saved 600 yuan. He'd spent 200 yuan on the train ticket. New shirt, 20 yuan, shoes, 60 yuan. He wanted to start afresh, as a new person.

He had 107 yuan left. He tried to give it to me, saying he wouldn't need it, but I told him to keep it. Then he asked me to get it to his wife and son. I said I would take care of it.

The police let me go with him to the station. In the police car, he said he wished I'd play a song for him on the radio. I broadcast his story and song on February 22, and I gave him the tape on February 24, before he was sent back to Sichuan.

I also gave him a dictionary and told him to study hard. I said he'd gotten in trouble because he was uneducated. He thought he might be too old to study, but I said an eighty-year-old man could learn and so could he. I told him that, if he wrote me, I would write back. One letter a week. He said that was too much, how about once a month?

Now he writes me every month from prison in Sichuan. He was sentenced to twelve years. Each letter is about one page, five or six hundred words. When other listeners learned of this, some started to write to him also, through me, including some college students. He's become pen pals with one college girl; they've exchanged five or six letters. He wrote me that he never expected to have a college student as a friend.

When I was in Sichuan on a business trip, I visited Gu Haijun in prison. First I went to see his family. I'd been in touch with his wife by phone, urging her to visit him and send him clothes and not have a change of heart. I'd found a lawyer for him. His family is very poor. Gu had been the main laborer and he'd been running for a decade. I got to his home at ten in the morning and his dad was already drunk. So I scolded the father, saying you are the head of the home, how can you behave like this? His dad makes some money by gathering and selling trash. His mom raises pigs and rabbits. His wife has some outside work. She gave me a pair of homemade shoes and a picture of the family to bring to him.

It was eight months since Gu and I had seen each other. He was so excited that he couldn't stop smiling. He was very clean, wore snow-white socks, looked very thin and handsome. At the visitors' office, he poured tea for me. I commented that he seemed to take the place as his home. He said, yes, he was used to it. He did not regret turning himself in because now he knew when he would get out; otherwise he would have faced the death sentence. He and his wife were counting the days. He said he watched TV, read newspapers, and wanted to help build a harmonious society.

I said he seemed more mature. Before, he had been living for himself; now he was beginning to have a sense of social responsibility.

After my broadcast about Gu Haijun, a listener in Shanxi sent me a message saying he wanted to walk the same road as Mr. Gu. I thought he was joking, because I'd gotten numerous messages from others claiming to be criminals that turned out to be pranks. I called him nevertheless. He told me that four years earlier he'd killed a man with whom his wife had an extramarital affair. I consulted a lawyer, who told me if the man turned himself in his life probably would be spared because his crime had some provocation. The caller and I kept in touch for a week, and then he suddenly showed up at the radio building. He was in rags. He'd changed buses four times and slept in the grass next to the highway. Now he's in prison for life.

Another listener, in Liaoning Province, sent me a message saying that, after hearing Gu's story, he'd given up a plan to kill his estranged wife and her parents.

Our program is not about law. But it does deal with preventing crimes, not doing crazy things, not killing people. Our influence is big, and not just on criminals. College listeners should feel they live happy lives because they are free. Migrant laborers might think they need to work on their bad tempers, because sometimes they have the killing instinct. The program is something between a news program and a psychiatric service—although a psychiatric service doesn't treat you like a friend. I've learned a lot from psychology experts. I must know enough to realize if callers are seriously ill and need to see a doctor.

Hosting a late-night talk program is hard. Not everyone can handle it. You have to have a sunny personality. I have the personality to handle it. I am independent. I like to make my own decisions. I make sure to exercise. I might look fragile from the outside, but I am very strong inside. I am open-minded. I can take in negativity and release it immediately. I also have a happy family and a good routine. I go to the movies once a week. I like to shop. I like hiking; I've climbed all the mountains around Beijing. I like to talk; my way to keep healthy is never hold anything in your heart, you must speak it out. At home, my husband is my garbage can! I talk to him over dinner. I let him talk too. When he is too quiet, I know something must be wrong. He listens to my program every day and understands me.

Actually my work mainly seems fun. I don't feel a lot of pressure. Radio listeners are loyal. They reward your work with sincerity, not necessarily with material things—although people have sent me gifts they think are valuable, and I think so too. Listeners have drawn portraits of me from their imagination—with glasses, or with curly hair. I have three or four such portraits in my home.

One of my listeners was a high school student from a poor grasslands area in Inner Mongolia. I advised him to stop listening to my program when he got to senior high, and promised that if he studied hard and got into a university in Beijing, I would go to the train station to pick him up. One day a package came from him, and inside was a bracelet of Buddha beads on a faded red string, obviously worn. The boy had gone to a temple to buy a token of safety and peace, seen this strand on the monk's wrist, and figured these beads had been blessed by the Buddha, since the seller always keeps the best for himself. So he asked the monk to sell him the beads, but the monk refused. He said how about giving them to me? The monk said, if I won't sell them, what makes you think I'd give them to you? The boy stayed at the temple and carried water for the monk for a whole day. The monk gave him the beads.

Another day I received a big box of dates, with no name or return address, just a postmark from a city in Hebei Province. I made a lot of calls and finally reached the farmer who sent them. Over the phone, I said this is Xiang Fei from China National Radio. I could sense his surprise. I thanked him for the dates. He said he grew them himself and he'd send me a box every autumn.

Our listeners' kindness is priceless to us. They ask for so little. They only want us to talk to them forthrightly and present good programs.

Journalism is a high-pressure job with a high casualty rate. You must be passionate to do the job well. I am crazy about radio, and I am a perfectionist. I don't do the job for the leaders of the radio station; I do it for my listeners. I don't have academic training in journalism, but I know what listeners want most. We must be truthful. We cannot fake anything. Our listeners are smart; they can tell whether you are genuine.

Since the Gu Haijun episode, I've gotten to know many more journalists and think some are damaging our reputation. A young woman from a magazine called my office and demanded I go downstairs to receive her in ten minutes. I had to ask who she was, and remembered I'd declined her earlier request for an interview because I didn't have time. She said she didn't want to interview me—she'd already written a 4,500-word article based on information from the Internet! She just wanted to take some pictures. I said I couldn't take the time, so she told me to e-mail her some pictures. I told her I didn't like her methods. I said, if she'd gotten material from the Internet for her article, couldn't she get photos from the Internet too? She said I really must be stuck up. I said I was sorry for interfering with her work but there were many other people worth writing about—why must you write about me? Then I hung up.

I decline as many interviews as possible, especially telephone interviews, which may come out all twisted. But I did oblige a young woman from a Hunan newspaper. She was insistent and said my director had already agreed. I told her to call me when I finished my program at 1:30 a.m., and I would give her twenty minutes on my way home. In fact, she hadn't talked to my director. Nevertheless, she took the trouble to call me at 1:30 in the morning, right on time. She said the criminal is a man and you are an attractive female host. I was disgusted and said, young lady, I want to explain something to you: Radio programs don't have video. I didn't know what he looked like, nor did he know what I looked like. Let's talk about something else. Then she asked about my husband. I asked her just what her angle was. She said she was asking the female host Xiang Fei from China National Radio to explain this beauty question to society.

I almost threw up blood on hearing this, I was so angry. When I got home, I asked my husband to go back upstairs while I stayed on the street talking to her. I said, young lady, I don't know your full name yet. I respect your commitment. But I am a journalist from national radio, while you are from a small provincial newspaper. If I wanted to explain something to society, would I need you to do it? If you wish to write from this perspective, you are letting me down. She said, since you are so mad, you must be hiding something. I was mad, but kept talking to her. I was out on the street until 3:30 a.m.—this was in February, very cold. I am older than you, I told her, and want to tell you a few things. You have good qualities. You are passionate for your work. But the basic requirement of journalism is truth. Don't go after sensation. It's the wrong road. One day you'll hit a wall.

At last she said, Sister Xiang Fei—it was the first time she called me sister—now I understand why Gu Haijun listened to you.

I said now I can go to sleep. If I hadn't said these things to you, I wouldn't have been able to sleep.

I'd asked her to give the article to my director to review after finishing it. She did and he said it was okay, no big problems.

Afterwards, she sent me a message asking me if I considered her a friend. I said of course. I asked her to bring me some Hunan duck necks if she came to Beijing—I knew if I didn't ask her for something, she would be reticent to come to see me, but this way she would feel obliged to come to see me.

I've supervised eight interns, college students and master's students. Only one did a satisfactory job. Another could work independently, but lacked depth.

I think journalism has acquired some kind of aura that is misleading to students. They all want to become famous overnight, but they don't want to work hard. They don't realize the importance of authentic communication.

The older generation of journalists might not know about MP-3 players or computers, but we have a lot to learn from them. Young journalists need to have a good attitude, and shouldn't try to take shortcuts. The smallest things reflect one's attitude. Learn to respect the people you interview. Never be late for an interview. One time an intern made an interviewee wait half an hour at the gate. I scolded her. She said she'd gotten caught in a traffic jam. I said that was no excuse. For today's interview with you, since I was unfamiliar with the location and heard it was hard to park, I came early. I told her never to be late again—better she wait than make others wait.

In the past when you turned on the radio, it was like listening to a teacher lecturing. Now radio is coming down from its lofty perch, down to earth, getting closer to listeners.

The reasons are many. One is ratings. If people don't like listening, there will be no listeners, and thus no commercials, and radio won't survive. This also brings problems; commercialism brings sensationalism. But for the most part, the main trend is good.

The media's influence is growing. In the past, media propagated. The direction was one way. Now media function as a monitor, to prevent bad things and spread good values. Journalism can increase openness, transparency, and justice. Media can provide a bridge between government and people.

I think things will only get better. It is like when I was in school, I had a bicycle, and felt happy. I never expected to own a car one day. When I got a motorcycle, I thought I'd reached the pinnacle. Now I have my own car. Development always exceeds our expectations.

V

NEW CONFIGURATIONS

· 18 ·

Wang Shuo
王 烁

Finance & Economics
财 经

$\mathcal{A}$ decade ago, after three years working as a night editor for *People's Daily*, a job he found dull, Wang Shuo signed on with a new business magazine, which became *Caijing*, meaning *Finance & Economics*. From its start in 1998, this publication has gone where others don't or won't, scrutinizing public affairs with depth and accuracy from the perspective of expertise, skirting overt politics and usually averting trouble—but not always: At least one 2006 issue was recalled from the printers to have some content replaced. A biweekly with a circulation said to be 80,000 in 2005, nominally affiliated with a government securities agency but privately financed and self-supporting, *Caijing* specializes in explanatory and investigative reporting. Its interests range from corporate governance to health, agriculture, and the environment, and it set the pace for coverage of SARS in 2003. The magazine is closely identified with its intrepid chief editor, Hu Shuli, now in her mid-fifties, who has said, "If a story is important enough, we'll find a way to talk about it." She referred us to Wang Shuo, two decades her junior, who presents himself as a quiet aide de camp merely following the boss's lead. Hu, on the other hand, makes it clear that the modest Wang plays a pivotal editorial and administrative role.

I was born in Sichuan Province, along the Red Water River, in a county bordering Guizhou Province, a place the Red Army passed through during the Long March. My parents are teachers. They graduated from college in 1966, on the eve of the Cultural Revolution, and returned to their hometown after graduation. I have two sisters, one back in Sichuan, the other living in France.

I never thought of being a journalist. I entered Renmin University in 1988, and hadn't done so well in the entrance exams, so I was assigned to the department of philosophy. I was surprised, but could do nothing about it. During my four years of college, I gradually became interested in philosophy, and thought this is heaven's will. I went on to graduate school in philosophy at Peking University, finishing in 1995. I needed a job. It's not easy for a philosophy student to find a job. So I decided to give up philosophy, and I sent my resume mostly to media organizations. One of them—the only one that offered me a job—was *People's Daily*. A total fluke. I was thrown into the journalism profession by life.

People's Daily surprised me. Many people see it as the mouthpiece of the Party, and think therefore it must be dreadful. Even though I found working there tedious, the people are very open-minded. But the place has its problems. I stayed three years, as a night shift editor, and quit in 1998, feeling I couldn't accomplish anything. Nobody would complain if you didn't do anything. But if you *did* things, for example, writing articles, it could bring on trouble. Not that anything I wrote dealt with sensitive topics—it's just that the environment has an attribute of inertia.

I almost took a job at *Southern Weekend*, and actually attended their annual work meeting in Guangzhou. But I stayed in Beijing after all, and joined a new magazine called *Qian (Money)*, the precursor of *Caijing (Finance & Economics)*. Our very first cover story was "Who is Responsible for Qiong Min Yuan?" That was the first company to be delisted from the stock market. The whole process took about a year. The founder was suspected of cheating, and the securities regulation commission lacked experience and hadn't done its job well. The general media had no interest in stock market news, while the media covering the stock markets were controlled by regulatory authorities and not allowed to cover this case. That left us a big space; other media didn't do it, but we did. That first issue sold 50,000 copies.

There was backlash: Under pressure from the securities regulation commission, *Money* magazine disappeared—but reappeared as *Finance & Economics*. I've been doing the same job from the start, although with different titles: I've been called executive editor, editing director, vice editor in chief, and managing vice editor in chief.

★   ★   ★

Media work gets redundant, and exciting moments fade with repetition. But one memorable story was the SARS epidemic. We were one of the earliest media outlets to cover it, beginning in April 2003. Our first article was about World Health Organization officials visiting Guangdong Province. It was not a big report, but in the process we learned the seriousness of SARS, and decided to report it fully. Our next issue had a cover story headlined "From Whence Comes the Danger?" with a picture of a mother wearing a mask, holding her daughter tightly, and looking at the camera with a frightened expression.

Where was the danger from? On the one hand, it came from SARS, and on the other it came from man-made disaster. At that time reporting about SARS required great courage, because the Ministry of Health had issued a report downplaying the threat, and the central government's attitude was ambiguous. Hu Shuli made the decision based on two points: First, this was a very important story, with too many people's lives threatened, so it was worth the risk. Second, she believed the central government didn't yet have adequate information, and would adjust its policy soon.

That issue came out April 21, and that same day the central government announced the removal of the health minister. This was coincidence, but noteworthy. Then Hu Shuli and two other reporters worked on a series in Shanxi Province tracing the sources of the epidemic. Hu showed an ability to make correct decisions in accordance with the times.

Our investigation of Guangxia, a company in the Ningxia Hui Autonomous Region that was listed on the Shenzhen and Shanghai stock exchanges, provides a model for investigative reporting in the economic field. Our reporter worked intensively on the story for three months, interviewing hundreds of sources and gathering evidence. It took us a long time to prove the company had been manipulating profit records for two years; it was actually losing money while its stock price increased eighty-fold. The company had won praise for planting Mahuang grass in Ningxia and helping to prevent desertification, and gotten visits from many central government officials, which provided a protective layer, albeit a very fragile one. At last we had enough proof that the company was faking its profits.

We published the story in August 2001. From first contact to publication took a year. The results were shockingly persuasive. The state commission regulating securities initiated an investigation immediately. The company's stock, billions worth, collapsed.

In the course of reporting this story, we never got pressure from the government. Rather, pressure came from the company, which had important people call us trying to prevent publication. This shows the power of commercial forces to intervene in the work of independent media, and that power has grown even stronger.

Another major story was the Shanghai pension fund scandal of 2006. We reported this even before Shanghai Party secretary Chen Liangyu was suspended and arrested. Other media focused on official corruption. But we felt there were huge problems in the management system of the pension fund, which had no monitoring or checks and balances. We reported the case from a systemic perspective, intertwined with an individual official's corruption and his fate. Again, this experience showed Hu Shuli's good judgment.

A Chinese saying goes: "If there is no light in the east, there is bound to be light in the west." There's no need to be discouraged; there are always things one can accomplish. If you get upset over one thing, you will miss many other opportunities.

People have different views on the media environment, some optimistic and others pessimistic, depending on their vantage point and milieu. There are three types of media in China. Some, like China Central TV, are part of the Party system, and subject to a large degree of government influence. Views from that environment are more pessimistic. The second type doesn't need financial support from the government, but relies on that system for personnel. For example, senior reporters from *Southern Weekend* came from *Southern Daily*, the Party newspaper of Guangdong Province. They are subject to less government influence, but still feel it. The third type is closest to independent; it needs only a license to publish from the government, but doesn't need financing or people. *Finance & Economics* is in this category.

The biggest difference between journalism and propaganda is in whom they represent. Party propaganda spreads ideology and promotes policy information to the masses. Commercial propaganda promotes products and images. The Party and enterprises represent the interests of a small number of people. Journalism belongs to the tradition of intellectuals, and represents the interests of the majority of society.

The quality of journalists is improving and they are more professional. We've hired people partly from other media, and some right out of school, including graduates from overseas. Many of our staff have studied in the United States. We specialize in economics, but we are journalists first. The territory is wide open for developing interesting stories. We like to do things that will involve the least intervention from the government and that can benefit the society in the longer term—so we've reported on law, public health, the environment, as well as business.

Finance & Economics is a place of professionals. Editors don't simply sit in their offices sending out commands. Our work is always a cooperative product between reporters and editors. Hu Shuli does her own reporting and writing. She is passionate about journalism, energetic, with ability to turn ideas into actions. She's had some difficult experiences. My experience is more comfortable—such as meeting with CEOs in my office. Hu provides a strong role model for us all. When SARS broke out, she wondered whether we should go in to work. I said if editors weren't in the office, the editing staff would fall apart. Sometimes we'll ask reporters to report on potentially dangerous events. But we don't require them to do life-threatening reporting. Some reporters were reluctant to report SARS, and I didn't force them.

Back in 1998, Hu Shuli had more experience than most economics reporters—and she'd only been in the field for two or three years. I had even less experience; in fact, none of us had much experience. We were among the earliest market-oriented media specializing in economic news. We dominated the field and there still are very few competitors. But the competitive landscape is changing. Many economics newspapers emerged after 2001. We have to respond rapidly, and cannot afford any delay in reporting important events. However, journalists must be confident that what they publish is correct. Most economic news media emphasize timeliness more than veracity. We think economic news should focus on veracity; we'd rather take more time to verify facts than hurry into print.

Today's rapid changes challenge conventional wisdom. They go beyond people's comprehension, even the comprehension of participants and decision-makers. A big change is diversity. There will be more and more opportunities and more layers. The community of market-oriented media will expand and provide soil for independent media to grow.

Journalists need to keep improving their professional skills. They also should be able to make clear value judgments as to right and wrong. Some colleagues say journalism should be separate from personal opinion. I respect this view, but the reality is that media are infused with value judgments of their producers.

Some say the chief editor determines the style of the media outlet. Others say it's a sign of immature media to have one person exert such strong control. From its establishment up to today, our magazine has been infused with Hu Shuli's judgment and personality, and I think that will remain the case for some time. Hu wants to have less influence, but it is not possible. When *Finance & Economics* becomes a weekly magazine in the future, and needs to be more systematic in operation, her individual influence may fade, and eventually life will go on without her, but the quality of the magazine will not be the same.

Young people who are interested in journalism should think carefully about going into this profession. Many Western journalists are happy because their line of work is their choice. They love reporting; if they didn't, they wouldn't choose it. Some Chinese journalists don't really love the profession, and it is not a choice of clear thinking. They are not happy. Once you enter, opportunities to leave are scarce. Benefits are limited. You might gain fame in a short time, but then the work gets repetitive. As time goes on, you may get disillusioned.

I don't have such feelings. I'm a calm person. I enjoy my work—although our cover story is unpredictable, so when I'm in charge of the cover story I sometimes do feel stressed. We don't consider the market when choosing the cover; nor are we influenced by advertising. We are editor-oriented. We decide what is important. But the decision to put which story on the cover often changes abruptly. In July 2005, the central bank decided to raise interests rates two percent. The decision was made on a Thursday night, so we replaced the cover story and did about thirty pages of reporting. I don't like working through the night. When the cover story is done and the pressure is off, I feel happy.

If I could choose my profession all over again, I don't know what I'd choose. It's not that I chose the wrong one, but neither can I say whether this one is right for me, or even if there is a right one for me.

Liu Zhouwei
刘 洲 伟

21st Century Business Herald
21 世 纪 经 济 报 道

$\mathcal{L}$iu Zhouwei is something of a wunderkind; since graduating from one of China's premier journalism programs, he's held a succession of editorial positions for a major newspaper industry group, culminating in his current post as chief editor of a paper that emulates the *Wall Street Journal*. Born in 1971, he's undoubtedly one of the youngest top editors of a national news outlet. Liu previously handled news and economics coverage in various capacities for the popular *Southern Weekend*. In 2000, he was tapped to help launch the *21st Century Business Herald* under the same parent company, the Guangzhou-based Southern Daily Group, boosted by private investment. The paper planned to go daily at the start of 2008. Liu bears his weighty responsibilities with evident good cheer; we were surprised he even found time to meet with us. He gave a spirited explanation of the demarcation between editorial and business operations at his paper—what Western publications call the "separation of church and state." He also mused, more than any other interviewee, about the long-term future of news and newspapers. While recognizing the key role of new technologies, he is adamant that people, talent, and experience are the foundation of a news organization's success, both journalistically and financially.

My background is nothing special; I was born into an ordinary family in a small county town near Luoyang, one of China's ancient capitals, in Henan Province. My mother became a rural teacher, and my father, a retired army officer, is now a local prosecutor.

I've always been interested in journalism. I started doing journalism in primary school—it was blackboard news back then. In high school and college, it was internally circulated mimeographed newsletters. I studied journalism formally at Renmin University, and graduated in 1994. I received some so-called professional training in journalism school, but from today's perspective it was insufficient. Journalism school only laid the foundation.

After working in the field for twelve years, I now have a lot of thoughts about being a journalist; but I recall no particular concern when I started out, just the feeling that I wanted to be a reporter. For a child growing up in the 1970s in a small isolated place, the media were your connection with the outside world. My family couldn't afford to travel, and I never left my hometown until college. So what I learned about the outside world was what I got through the media. In childhood, I already had the idea that efforts in the media could have some impact; you might not be able to change anything or determine anything, but over time your work could have strong influence. In the late 1980s, the media were especially active, and even in a backwater you could feel their radiating power and values. For children, media represented a kind of enlightenment. For grownups, media shaped life decisions. That was the situation through my high school years, when one's outlook is gradually forming.

For about six months during college, in 1993, I did an internship at *China Youth News*. The paper was very lively at the time and gave interns lots of opportunities. It had several weekly supplements, for economics, culture, and society; while I was there, the editor in charge of the societal supplement did an April Fools issue that got him removed from the position. My first reporting was for a series of stories about sandstorms in Beijing and other environmental issues. The practical training at work felt more effective than learning theories in school; you were out in the field, determining topics, writing articles, and receiving feedback. It was exciting and gave you a sense, physically as well as mentally, of growing abilities and power—like *gongfu* martial arts practitioners whose joints are crackling in growth in the middle of the night, that sort of collection of energy.

Upon graduation in 1994, I was recruited by *Southern Weekend*, which was in the process of transforming into a serious newspaper—comparable to what a paper like *The New York Times* went through in an earlier period. *Southern Weekend* had been considered "yellow," not in the sense of pornographic, but rather sensationalistic, with lots of anecdotes and freaky stuff intended to amuse readers. But during the early 1990s, it was becoming China's most influential paper of societal news, concerned with public opinion, the lower classes, and especially the weak and poor.

I worked as vice director of *Southern Weekend*'s Beijing bureau, mainly in charge of news, for three years, and as the paper's overall deputy director of news for another three years. After that I helped launch the paper's economic news department and switched to economics reporting for about a year.

Southern Weekend was truly a training ground. In addition to its humanistic concerns and passions, the paper considers what readers want, and makes selections and decisions in accordance with readers' needs. Furthermore, it looks for stories with impact. Young journalists who work there know that the paper first of all must be successful in the marketplace to gain respect as a news outlet. So they actually accept two different kinds of education: On the one hand, they concern themselves with the masses and pursue journalistic ideals on behalf of China's suffering and oppressed people. On the other hand, they must produce readable stories conveying the drama along with the essentials of the news, paying great attention to writing style with the purpose of selling the paper.

During that period, we watched the sales of each issue closely. If sales went down, everyone was dejected. If sales went up, everyone was overjoyed. We accepted this sort of market consciousness along with journalistic consciousness, and the two blended in an unusual way as China's market developed. Opportunities arose from this mixture, including the opportunity to launch the *21st Century World Economic Herald*.

We built it from a bankrupt newspaper in Guangzhou. Legally speaking, newspapers in China were not considered commercial enterprises and the notion of bankruptcy didn't apply to them; but in any case, this paper couldn't go on. It was called the *Guangdong Jiage Bao* (*Guangdong Pricing News*), with a small staff of seven or eight, and operated by the provincial price control bureau, which set prices before market controls came in. The management offered the publication license at a very low price to the Southern Daily Group, whose leaders took it as a chance to let young people develop a new media outlet. We didn't want their personnel; we only wanted their license, and they only wanted payment. It was a swap of their publication number in exchange for 300,000 yuan, a very simple deal.

So after seven years with *Southern Weekend*, I started planning the new paper. We applied to the State Press and Publications Administration for approval to publish under the new name, *21st Century World Economic Herald,* referring to the new century and our hope that the paper could go on reporting economic news for one hundred years. When they got our application, they were a little dubious: Gee, isn't this too wordy for the name of a newspaper? But we insisted on this name.

We wanted to become something like the *Wall Street Journal*. We hatched our plan in the summer of 2000, started trial issues in October 2000, and, after four trial issues, officially launched the paper on New Year's Day of 2001. The central propaganda department had issued circular number fifty-one, permitting market-oriented newspapers, which enabled us to accept private investment. Although Southern Daily Group has done well, at that time funds were tight. So we brought in the Shanghai Fuxing Group, one of China's biggest private industrial and venture capital groups, as a minority shareholder.

We began with four people, all from *Southern Weekend*—myself from economic news, my successor as head of the news department, the deputy manager of the ad department, and the deputy head of a supplement. It was a top-tier team. But we had one constraint: We were not allowed to bring along anybody from our former departments, not even a single reporter. So we had to recruit staff.

After the launch, I visited Beijing and Shanghai to lure people from among my friends and journalism contacts. I told them that, as a market-directed media outlet, we probably would offer better pay and handsome bonuses. I told them the culture was straightforward: If they wrote more, they'd get promoted, and if they wrote well, they'd get important positions. I pointed out that, since economics was a new specialty for media, we had a blank slate and plenty of space for rapid growth, as well as a good platform for individuals to shine. In Beijing alone, with the snap of a finger, I pried twenty or thirty people away from other newspapers.

At that time, China only had a few mainstream economics publications: *Caijing (Finance & Economic)*, which had just started, *Zhonghua Gongshang Shibao (China Business Times)*, which was going downhill, and a couple more papers. In our assessment, we didn't face much competition. We thought that as long as we organized a good team we could prevail in about three years—reach number one on whatever criterion, be it circulation, influence, advertising revenue, or reporting network.

We don't really consider the older government-run papers, *Jingji Ribao (Economic Daily)* and *Jingji Cankao Bao (Economic Reference News)*, competition at all, since they still get government subsidies and their circulation is artificially sustained by administrative order rather than voluntary subscriptions. There also are some publications with niche monopolies, mainly reporting on securities and aimed at banks and financial institutions. They operate in a different realm and have special permits that we cannot get.

From that initial staff of four, we have grown to about 240 people in editorial. If you include advertising, circulation, and administration, the workforce totals nearly four hundred. Our biggest office is in Beijing, with seventy or eighty reporters and twenty or thirty in advertising and management. We also have a big office in Shanghai. Under China's newspaper management system, licenses cannot freely be moved about, so our headquarters is still in Guangzhou.

At our paper, editors and reporters are completely separated from advertising and circulation personnel. Like in the United States—they don't use the same elevator, right? We set up systematic firewalls. That means advertising personnel cannot contact reporters. If they do and get found out, they'll face punishment. I'm in charge of the news-editorial side, while the general manager oversees the business side. The two are clearly divided. On a management level, of course, the general manager and I talk, mainly about budget issues. Every year I need 50 million yuan worth of news coverage, so I must bargain with him. I tell him he can't give me too little while he says I can't ask for too much. We negotiate.

Our paper also is like an American newspaper in having shareholders and a directorate. Once at a board meeting, the general manager made accusations against me, saying Liu Zhouwei's news department always gets us into trouble that loses us as much as 30 million yuan in advertising income. I admitted this was so, but said he was mixing up two different issues. Our reporting can't just gloss over a company's bad doings for the sake of advertising.

A good company should take criticism seriously, but some companies are simply bad. Half of China's publicly traded stock companies are in this category. They might be rich, but their money came from fraud and exploitation of shareholders. You can't be nice to them; you must report on them. Other companies are good but have done bad things, or perhaps some of their managers at times were muddleheaded. In such cases, you still can't say I won't report on this because it's a good company. We are vigorous in exposing bad behavior. Sometimes we trace fundamental problems to their system and corporate management structure. When we do so, the reaction often is: How come whenever they expose us, they reach down to the roots?

We transmit by satellite and print the paper at a dozen sites nationwide. In Beijing we've subcontracted with *People's Daily* to print for us; they also transport the paper directly to the market in Beijing and the whole of North China—Shijiazhuang, Tianjin, and other cities. We come out three times a week—we put the paper together on Monday, Wednesday, and Friday and sell it Tuesday, Thursday, and Saturday.

We have three types of readers. Type one is China's political elite. Type two is China's business elite. Type three is China's intellectual and cultural elite. Ordinary workers and peasants don't read our paper. At two yuan a copy, the paper might be too expensive for them. And they can't understand it anyway. Our hope is that, through creating this platform aimed at our core readership, the three kinds of elites, we can foster communication, formation of public opinion, and creation of consensus, and eventually push China forward. I don't know if we should call it evolution or progress.

I cannot really disclose our circulation figures—there are no neutral authentication agencies, so I don't know what to say. There is a common understanding in our industry that, when you publish circulation figures in China, such numbers are just a game. For instance, when our advertising people and circulation people go out and tell people in the trade that our paper has a circulation of 520,000 copies, and other papers say they have such and such a circulation, none of these is the real circulation. If you put out a number, the competition just provides a bigger number. I don't want to give you a figure and then have our competition say their circulation is much bigger. In fact there is a number and we definitely know it well. I can tell you that our circulation ranks number one.

Our paper's rapid development has created new competitors who then lure away the talent we've cultivated. That's what we did before, and now it's the turn of others to do it to us. The new startups like *Diyi Chaijing Ribao* (*First Finance & Economics Daily*), *Chaijing Shibao* (*Finance & Economics Times*), *Guoji Jinrong Bao* (*International Finance News*), and others are only so-so. But each new paper steals away a batch of our people with much higher salaries. The Internet companies have even more money—big ones such as Sina, Sohu, and Netease have U.S. investment and can ignore costs when they go after our people. I'll mentor a young reporter fresh out of school, and three years later, when he has acquired a reputation, an Internet company will lure him away as a chief editor, paying him three to four times what we can. Most of our reporters are fairly young—twenty-seven or twenty-eight on average. Young people have their priorities: they want to get married and buy apartments. There is very little we can do about it.

It's hard to say how long this situation will last. Meanwhile it drags down the level of our industry. The vitality of our paper rests completely on our editors and reporters. Many of the editors, including me, are young, and the reporters are even younger. To develop a paper into something like the *New York Times* or *Wall Street Journal*, you must cultivate a batch of elite newspaper people who form the newspaper's institutional memory over the long term. This requires constant accumulation generation by generation. Now, no sooner have you collected talent than it gets whisked away, and you collect some more and it gets diluted again. It's an agonizing problem.

But this is not our biggest challenge. Our biggest challenge is the uncertainty of the future of print media. This is a quandary for our friends in America as well. What will the mainstay of the media of the future be? What is the growth potential for newspapers? Can print continue to play the role it has played for readers in the past? Fewer and fewer young people read newspapers. They use the Internet and their cell phones. The Internet and cell phones shall become their portals to the world. Who will read newspapers then? Those successful young people who will be opinion leaders ten years from now will be accustomed to browsing the Internet. My colleagues don't read other newspapers, either; if they want to find out what other papers are doing, they go to the Internet.

We still want to do journalism and we still cherish journalistic ideals. But those of us who write news for publication to reach readers have to think differently. The newspaper is merely a medium; it's not the news itself. What we do is news, not newspapers. News doesn't have to be printed on paper; it can be published via the Internet or some other medium. I use a metaphor to talk about this: I say we need a platform for our journalism like Jesus needed a church. Not having a platform is like not having the church. Then how can you go on preaching and sermonizing and influencing others?

When we started the paper, we expected China to join the World Trade Organization in a few months—which did happen. What's the significance of China joining the WTO? It means China is willing to accept and conduct itself according to the global rules of the game. It means great development for business and great changes in the rules of business as well. We're not talking about socialism and capitalism. We're talking about a true transformation from planned economy to market economy. When you agree to join WTO, you must accept the market system. This system will thoroughly transform Chinese society. It will lead to the emergence of a middle class. We set out to observe these profound changes in the business world and meanwhile probe into political, social, and cultural results of these changes.

Sometimes we organize forums of corporate and government decision makers and influential scholars and give space to their speeches promoting changes in certain areas—for instance, what to do about foreign exchange rates. This projects our influence. Zhongnanhai, the compound of the Communist Party and central government leadership, has subscriptions for several hundred copies of our paper.

A project we did on capital markets in 2002 had quite an impact. The story was headlined "Knock Things Down and Start Over," and forecast that in the next few years the Chinese stock market would face great changes and needed to be overhauled. Sure enough, in the next three years, the stock market kept dropping. Our report drew the attention of high-level decision makers and led to some changes thereafter in the market. We also were the first to publish the "Lang Xianping vs. Gu Chujun debate," a controversy over China's ownership transformation and the inevitability of exploitation of some by some others, which subsequently turned into a big issue on the Internet.

Which raises another problem of the Internet—they use stuff originally written by others to generate a huge volume of follow-up postings. So they take our stuff and get as many as two hundred thousand postings in a month.

A newspaper can't possibly carry so many readers' letters. But on the Internet, presto, public opinion wells up and politicians must respond. Still, it's very satisfying to know your job of good reporting actually produced significant change. As a result of these controversies, the policy of privatizing state-owned enterprises through management buyouts was reversed. That original ownership transformation was the basis of many private companies. Now MBOs have been banned. This has huge implications for remaining state-owned enterprises and the development of private companies.

Personally, I believe in gradual reformation. Once you lay down a good foundation, you should move ahead one step at a time. You shouldn't always try to make revolution. China has seen many revolutions, but in the end none have turned out ideal. You have to accept social realities; you can't possibly wipe out real conditions and create a utopia according to romantic ideas. And in my opinion, more than two hundred years of Chinese history has proven that utopianism is harmful. I want our reporters and editors to look at issues rationally. You should look for problem-solving methods instead of just raising questions. And when you ask questions, you should think about how to solve them. What should be the optimal solution under the constraints?

We are under the supervision of the propaganda department, but I don't know anything about propaganda, as I've never done it. I think the fundamental tenets of journalism are the same everywhere: accuracy, objectivity, timeliness, such basic requirements. Furthermore, you must have your own values and must be vigilant about your values. When you write and edit for the paper, you should be as objective as possible. And at a trade medium like ours, you cannot do without a store of specialized knowledge. We are getting fewer and fewer reporters with a journalism background. The best is if they have two degrees, one in journalism and one in another area, such as law, political science, banking, insurance, or management. I myself am enrolled in an executive MBA program.

The greatest change in Chinese journalism since I entered the field is the advent of more and more market-oriented newspapers, and more and more of them are doing journalism according to business rules. This wasn't possible before. In the past, one could only talk about journalistic ideals. Now we also talk about IPOs and getting listed on the stock exchange. The benefit of market orientation is financial independence. In the past budgets were allocated from above, money was always tight, and you couldn't travel at will. Nobody took planes to go gather news; even the most experienced reporters had to take trains. Now even our most ordinary reporters go around by air.

Because we had the financial means, when SARS came, we could organize a team of more than twenty journalists focusing on SARS coverage. It was very costly—we spent several million yuan. That would have been unimaginable without financial resources. Technically, the more freedom we achieve financially, the more space we acquire for reporting.

Another benefit of marketization is higher earnings for journalists. Our reporters don't get fixed salaries; we pay according to the quality and quantity of reporting, which makes people work harder. A rank-and-file reporter at our paper now can make 20,000 yuan in a good month. That, too, was unthinkable before.

The downside is that commercial interests can interfere with freedom and independence of the press. I've heard about other papers succumbing to pressure from advertisers. That firewall against commercial forces is necessary if a newspaper is to have credibility.

And there's the problem of rapid growth drawing more capital as others emulate your mode, so the whole industry gets spread too thin, and everyone focuses on low-level competition rather than on creativity and raising standards.

But I think the pros outweigh the cons, and we're still healthy.

We hope to take our paper daily in 2008. We need a better interactive website. We also hope that in the next two to three years we will be able to find a new medium in addition to print. Eventually we hope to become a business and journalism group, to develop into something like a Dow Jones or Reuters. At the same time, I hope our editors and reporters become more mature and professional. They are not good enough and still have a long way to go to catch up with *Wall Street Journal* reporters. They must catch up.

You've asked good questions. You should ask me if I have children. I have two. My daughter was born when the paper was being launched. I feel like I've missed her childhood, so now I spend time with her every day. She'll start primary school later this year. It was a great pity that I missed the period between birth and age six. Of course my wife complained; when I got home she'd scold me so much it felt like a pot of dog blood being poured over my head. My wife and I were college schoolmates and she used to be a magazine editor but I asked her to stay home when we had kids. Once they're both in school she'll be liberated again.

Zhang Lixian
张 立 宪

Reader's Warehouse
读 库

$\mathcal{W}$hen we met with Zhang Lixian, he came across as gleeful as a new father. He'd published two issues of a creation that seemed to be the perfect outcome of a peripatetic career, and was working on the third. He subsequently completed a full year's run of the bimonthly *Duku, Reader's Warehouse*, primarily a nonfiction literary journal in book format—what some call a "mook"—and continued with the 2007 series. In between, he put out a special issue opening with photographs of readers' babies born the same year as his brainchild, with accompanying essays extending the metaphor. Zhang's background combines the conventional and the offbeat: He went from stable predictability at a provincial Party paper to aimless freelancing in Beijing, then to a secure job in publishing that got him official residency in Beijing so his family could join him, before plunging into his independent venture. His publication carries an eclectic mix of arts, culture, history, and miscellany, and he prides himself on scrupulous concern for both design and content. He does everything from start to finish—commissioning and editing articles and essays, obtaining ISBN numbers for each issue, contracting for printing, and managing distribution by subscription and through bookstores, all the while maintaining a lively interactive presence on the web. When we sat down to talk at a Beijing teahouse, he'd just come from the post office and was toting a carton, the latest unsolicited gift from an appreciative reader.

~

Beijing is my spiritual hometown. I spent my college years in Beijing; my friends and former schoolmates are in Beijing; and my most important period of growing up was in Beijing. So in 1997, after six years working at the *Hebei Daily*, the Party paper of Hebei Province, I told my employer that I wanted to return to Beijing for graduate school. That was just the pretext; in fact, I was determined to move to Beijing, and, had they not agreed, I would have resigned. But they did agree and gave me a two-year leave of absence. From the bottom of my heart, I really hoped that in two years I would be able to tell them I no longer wanted to return.

I enrolled in graduate studies at Renmin University, and with my college training and work experience completed the program fairly easily, but for a while I was doing poorly. At the peak of my difficulties, I was taking a course on Marxist journalism theory. I left an exam feeling dejected, and when I exited the school gate I saw street peddlers selling fake diplomas and thought that, if I flunked out of school, I could buy a fake diploma as a last resort. In the end, it turned out I'd done fine on the exam.

In my two years at Renda, 1997 to 1999, I actually devoted more energy to moonlighting than to schoolwork. I didn't even live in the dorms; I rented an apartment. My friends provided me with lots of opportunities. First I went over to China Central TV to help a college friend produce a program on soccer. The program wanted to put out a magazine, so I took charge of that—*Zuqui Zhiye* (*Soccer Night*), which reached a huge circulation its first year, selling 50,000 to 100,000 copies. I also did some work for a precursor of *Beijing News*, which invited me to oversee publication of a special paper in conjunction with the 1998 World Cup in France. We published *Shijiebei Kuaibao* (*World Cup Bulletin*) for forty days, with circulation rising from 7,000 at the launching to about 100,000 at the conclusion.

Those two years were critical for me. I was providing services in a market, and gradually learning market principles. My concepts of writing, editing, and interviewing also changed a great deal.

I had enough work to live as a kind of drifter in Beijing. Still, the decision to stay was hard. I was married, my family was in Shijiazhuang, and I had an apartment and my status as an employee at *Hebei Daily* there. My final choice probably had to do with my age: I was twenty-eight when I returned to Beijing, and didn't want to live a life whose every step was predictable unto death. If I stayed at *Hebei Daily*, by thirty-five I'd become a department head, and by forty or forty-five an editorial board member, and, if I did even better, the outcome at best would be chief editor. I could almost see my life through to the end. Such a life would lack freshness and suspense.

So I told *Hebei Daily* that I wouldn't return after my graduate studies. But I didn't break off with them completely; my affiliation, my dossier, my residency remained in Shijiazhuang. I continued freelancing and thinking up projects in Beijing.

In the summer of 2000, I got the idea to develop a book around a Hong Kong movie, *Dahua Xiyou* (*Big Talk About "Journey to the West"*). Although the movie hadn't done that well at the box office, it had become the focus of a trend: Young people were discussing it on the Internet and starting websites about it. At that time, the mainstream publishing industry hardly paid any attention to this sort of popular cultural phenomenon. I thought it had potential, so I masterminded a volume around the movie and its aftermath, with tales from behind the scenes, tracing how the fad had emerged among young people in China. This book sold 200,000 copies.

The publisher, Modern Times Publishing House, was impressed and offered me an editing job. It's a government company, part of the China Publishing Group. I'd never imagined that, after three years of drifting, I'd go back to working for a mainstream, state-owned organization! The company transferred my residency and dossier, and those of my wife, to Beijing. From 2000 to 2004 I was deputy chief editor for this publishing house.

But I still felt a widening gap between that kind of work and my editing concepts and views. So in 2004 I left the company and drifted around again for more than a year.

Then I got a new idea to put out a literary journal-cum-book. I published number 0600 of *Duku* (*Readers Warehouse*) in the fall of 2005 to test the market. The response was positive. So I decided to follow up in 2006 with six books, numbered 0601 to 0606, and the following year six more, 0701 to 0706, and so on. Response to the first issue of 2006 was even better than I expected; after 10,000 sold I had to do another printing of 5,000 more.

In the United States people have coined the term "mook" for this sort of publication; we use the transliteration and also call it *muke* in Chinese. China actually has quite a few now—such as *Lao Zhaopian* (*Old Photos*) and *Jinri Xianfeng* (*Today's Vanguard*), and a series including *Jingjixuejia Chazuo* (*Economists' Teahouse*) and *Shehuixuejia Chazuo* (*Sociologists' Teahouse*) published in Shandong. It's a mixed product, published in book format with an ISBN number, but also like a magazine in being issued periodically and continuously. My publication doesn't contain ads, and it's priced at thirty yuan. In theory, you cannot subscribe; it's sold in bookstores.

My concept comes out of my professional background as a newspaper journalist who later transferred to a publishing company. Over the years, I'd noticed that friends and writers around me had medium-length manuscripts on their hands, probably between 5,000 and 50,000 characters, too long for newspapers and magazines but too short to constitute a book. My readers' warehouse idea could serve as a platform for these mid-length reads.

My hope was that writers would spend time and energy to cover subjects from last year or the year before that still had value from today's point of view. The book format, first, would not be so time-bound. Second, the sales cycle of the book form would be longer. Third, the contents would stand the test of time and not be as fragile as news.

As the editor, I handle everything from organizing, selecting stories, and working with the writers to cover design, paper selection, contracting with printers, circulation, and promotion. Having studied journalism and acquired fifteen years in this profession, I've found myself working to counteract much of my education and experience. I think my background actually makes it harder to arrive at elementary knowledge—so only now can I learn the simplest principles and regain some common sense.

For instance, my generation didn't receive enough aesthetic education; we have a poor sense of color and pattern and poor understanding of what is beautiful or ugly. People think a book cover must be garish to draw attention. I now believe that, in designing a book, you should trust the eyes of the reader and at the same time respect his eyes. By trust, I mean that the reader can tell a good book from a bad book. By respect, I mean that you shouldn't overstimulate.

Over the years, and on the basis of our reading experiences from an early age, we've also formed erroneous concepts about language. As an editor, I would agonize about whether the written language we often read is the same one used by the great classic authors Li Bai and Du Fu. Why are things we write today so unreadable? Gradually I developed new understandings. We emphasize adjectives and rarely use verbs. We use exaggeration and ornamental terms. We make generalizations, and don't use enough detail, data, and facts.

I have specific conditions for manuscripts now, such as avoiding exclamation marks, omitting superlatives, and removing redundant adjectives like "respected old man"—if your article is well written, then the reader automatically knows in his heart that this old man is worthy of respect, or, if he isn't, the reader can decide. I sum up my requirements with one sentence: Lay bare the facts, but do not impose opinions. Five years back, I still wrote and edited articles that forcibly guided the reader to a particular viewpoint, but now I think that's wrong. I believe that viewpoints, concepts, appraisals, conclusions all belong to the reader. You should not deprive the reader of his right and his pleasure to come to a conclusion. Nor should you deprive the reader of his right and pleasure to come up with his contrary conclusion.

★   ★   ★

I've always liked an ancient story from China's Spring and Autumn period, that goes something like this: In 607 B.C., the ruler of the State of Jin was planning to kill his prime minister, Zhao Dun. On hearing the news, Zhao Dun escaped from the capital, and, in his absence, his nephew organized and carried out a plot to kill the king instead. Hearing of the successful assassination, Zhao Dun returned to discover that Jin's official historiographer, Dong Hu, had recorded that Zhao Dun was the assassin. Zhao Dun lodged a protest, to which Dong Hu replied that, as the official in charge of the country, Zhao Dun indeed was responsible for the king's death. After having the historiographer killed, and then the son who succeeded him killed, eventually Zhao Dun relented and took the blame.

We can learn a lot from this story. The recorder—who was a reporter, after all—was courageous and responsible. A journalist must have courage, which can be manifested in conduct or merely in the word used to summarize an event. But sometimes it is not all about courage. For instance, even if policies allow you to write and to report factually, how can you ensure that you are truthful? If you still write stuff full of exclamation marks and opinions, is that truthful? Nobody limits you, but technical details are a barrier to truth.

China's media professionals lack clear concepts for editing; instead we are changeable, swaying left and right. Another problem is lack of resolve and a tendency toward capitulationism. We give in to the market and to conventions in the industry, instead of implementing new styles and ideas.

I'm not trying to implement big theories; I just want to implement small technical things, including how an editor should communicate with a writer, which in reality is quite a challenge. A very good writer can write about anything she likes and it can go directly to press. Other than fixing some typos, little communication is required. With another writer, the relationship requires supervision and control and interactivity.

Take the first story in the first issue of 2006, which runs seventy-eight pages, about Guo Degang, a performer of *xiangsheng*—Chinese "crosstalk," comic monologues and dialogues performed with rapid-fire delivery. The author is an amateur writer who loves folk arts. I helped him weed out the usual defects from his interviews, such as mixing in too much personal opinion. I also asked him to validate and confirm every single detail: What was the subject wearing? What was he holding? Whom did he call? How long did it take him to get here? He wrote 40,000 characters and I condensed it to 30,000, editing word by word.

Our decision to do this story was serendipitous. The writer had been a fan of Guo Deguang for three years, attending his crosstalk performances in the days when they might draw an audience of three or four people. I thought Guo was quite good, but he was little known when I assigned the story. The author spent about three months interviewing and writing. The first two months were freewheeling chats. But in the middle of the writing, Guo suddenly became the subject of media hype, and by the time the story was finished, Guo had become very popular. By the time the book came out, after spring festival, there'd been more than a thousand media reports on him.

That's the way it is now; everybody follows the fads. As soon as someone possesses star effect, all the media join in the hype. But this was a lucky coincidence. Of all the others who interviewed Guo, I believe that nobody spent more than a week with him, but we spent three months, and before that our reporter had been in his audience for three years.

In my opinion, China's media is insufficiently diverse. We publish probably hundreds of millions of pages every day, but the content is limited. Political stars, academic stars, and entertainment stars occupy most of the space. These celebrities by and large have been tapped to the point where they no longer talk like humans. The truly valuable stories are not about these stars. Most media don't dare risk doing something else; it's safest to stick to movie directors like Zhang Yimou and Chen Kaige, actress Zhang Ziyi, famous scholar Yu Qiuyu, and our politicians. But those neglected by the media have the most to offer. They are the people I wish to introduce.

The greatest challenge I face is being resolute about my own editing principles and judgments. I myself wavered in developing my publication, because I know lots of celebrities. I could do Chen Kaige. I could get manuscripts from Yu Qiuyu. But by not aiming for the big mass audience, and instead publishing for more specialized audiences, you still can win strong resonance from a lot of people. There are always going to be more people who never hear about a book, or who don't like and won't buy it, than people who know, like, and buy the book. Otherwise, wouldn't my book sell 1.3 billion copies? Why can I sell only 10,000 copies? You should try to win over those who never hear of, don't like, and don't buy, but first of all you should serve those in your circle—which might be good enough.

I adhere to the concept of smaller and fewer, which is unusual in this trade. In China, we tend to pursue blind expansion. When we do something, we want to grow big and powerful, and only then do we deem it a success. City planners take pride in the width and number of streets; they consider wider streets and more streets signs of modernization. Decision makers in media also worship scale. When a newspaper is profitable, it will launch a bunch of new periodicals that basically are similar. If it were up to me, I would use the money to enhance people's abilities and improve the existing paper, rather than adding carriages to the car. But most decision-makers will revel in the fact that their single paper has now developed into a press group owning more than ten newspapers and several magazines.

★   ★   ★

In the past, we were taught to consider journalism a tool for indoctrination. People were embarrassed or scared to talk about the commodity nature of media: A book, a newspaper, a magazine are commodities and should be sold for money. This view is no longer controversial—but how to sell? It's easy to say that you want to put out a readable and profitable newspaper, but our schools and the industry as a whole haven't taught us how to realize such goals on an operational level. Change will be up to our generation and younger generations.

I think the biggest change in Chinese media in the past ten years is the strengthening of a consciousness of providing service. This in turn is built on a sense of equality with readers. Chinese journalists used to have illusions based on how they were treated; when they went out reporting, people gave them respect, and sometimes flattery and presents and bribes. This easily could distract a young person from the essence of the profession; he might take journalism as a tool for making money, satisfying his vanity, solving his problems in life and opening up doors. This basically was my situation at *Hebei Daily*. I didn't have to worry about anything. If someone in my family needed hospitalization, our health reporters could help me contact doctors. If the police took away my driver's license, the public security reporter could get it back. Journalism became a kind of resource to cash in for self-interest.

How did I change? I broke out of the matrix and came to Beijing to be a hired hand. I had to please editors and write good stuff that readers would appreciate. It was a difficult transformation. I had to give up my airs and run about making a living like an ordinary person. Once you and your readers share the same footing, you no longer feel superior. Now, as an editor, I cannot help thinking about how to make things appealing and worth readers' money. This transformation is not just my own; gradually, all professionals in our vocation are going through this change. The only differences are that some feel it more keenly while others are a bit more passive, and some are clearer about specific methods while others are still pondering what to do.

I write about my editing experience in my blog, so many readers have watched my publication grow up. It's like watching someone's growth process from birth to adulthood: You may not be a blood relation, but you are still happy for him. My readers promote my book in their own blogs and websites and through their contacts at newspapers, without me even knowing about it.

I would say I am under great economic pressure. I paid the printer for my first issue, but sales take two to three months, and only then do I get payment, and even then I might not. In my first half-year of efforts, I still haven't seen any economic returns. But I don't feel I'm making a sacrifice. I greatly enjoy the process—the pleasure and enjoyment far exceed the problems. City life can be pallid and boring. But the process of putting out this book series opened up a huge new world for me. I've met people scattered among different vocations and different localities who share aspirations and interests with me. A reader in a small county seat somewhere in South China will send me a whole year's payment before she's even seen what the book is like. Nor does she know who I am. She sends me a letter, 10,000 characters long, describing her job-hunting experience and her feelings about it. This sort of trust and loyalty are of great value and enrich my life.

I think any publication should bring rewards in three areas—intellectual, technical, and emotional. The intellectual aspect means the content, including writing style. Technical refers to appearance, including binding and layout, paper, and printing. Emotional is the relationship among readers, writers, and editors. The greatest reward for me from my publication is the emotional consolation. This project was accomplished in a relatively extreme manner, and brings forth extreme love and extreme hate. A reader may express his liking in a relatively extreme manner as well. For instance, he'll pay thirty yuan to buy the book, and he'll thank me for it, and then he might send me a pack of tea worth seventy yuan! This is the emotional content he brings to you. Readers send me gifts—one just sent me this box with salt-preserved duck. I hope I can continue to progress and live up to this preserved duck.

Afterword

Christopher Merrill
Director, International Writing Program, The University of Iowa

$\mathcal{A}$ Chinese proverb invoked in this collection of interviews—that you cannot recognize the true face of Mount Lushan from within the mountains—has a corollary for outsiders attempting to find in the changing face of China some familiar features: You will not find your way through the mountains without a native guide. And there are no better guides to contemporary China than journalists who came of age in the wake of the government crackdown on the 1989 protests in Tiananmen Square.

What these journalists reveal, in their conversations with Judy Polumbaum and Xiong Lei, are not only the particular demands of their craft but also the textures and contours of a culture in the midst of historic change.

To extend the metaphor: The path keeps disappearing, and so we turn to those whose knowledge of the terrain, curiosity, and courage to ask sometimes difficult questions may uncover new routes to the interior.

It is a common story: A closed society opens, what was once forbidden becomes commonplace, and as the authorities seek to control forces that are inherently unstable—flows of capital or information, for example—men and women yearn for truth as much as or more than for freedom. And what is inscribed in their daily lives is the stuff of journalism no less than the stories and scandals ferreted out of the darkened corridors of power, as these journalists illustrate in their expert navigation of this rising power.

One comment by Jin Yongquan of the *China Youth News* may stand for the virtues of this book: "Reporting from the countryside made me understand a plain truth—that when it comes to social relations in China, if you can open one link in a chain, it becomes possible to open all the links."

No outsider can open those links with the dexterity of an enterprising insider; hence it is critical to understand how these journalists view their journeys to their respective vantage points—the nature of their training; the shifting roles they play; the complications of censorship; their accommodations to the market; the political, economic, social, and other environmental forces shaping their work. These men and women indeed are telling the most important story of our time.

Iowa City
December 2007

Acknowledgments

$\mathcal{M}$y debts of gratitude are many. Those due thanks include, for heroic translation assistance, Gao Yuan, Zhang Zhaohui, and Li Xiao; for early readings and suggestions, Steve Berry, Jennifer Hemmingsen, Julie Kearney, Li Xing, and Stephen Vlastos; for two rounds of meticulous copyediting, the unparalleled JoAnn Castagna; and for assistance with long-distance communications and final calibrations, the ever-dependable Mao Xiulin.

The University of Iowa provided backing in various forms, including a Faculty Scholar Award, related support from the Office of the Provost, and grants from the Iowa Arts & Humanities Initiative and the Center for Asian & Pacific Studies; the indomitable Brenda Gritsch and Phyllis Rosenwinkel of Iowa's School of Journalism & Mass Communication processed the unending paperwork. As Iowa students, Johan Bergenas and Susan Hills rendered help through the undergraduate scholar assistant program.

Aryeh Neier, having been accosted by a total stranger who said she'd be sending him a work-in-progress in the hopes he'd consider writing a foreword, responded swiftly and elegantly. Christopher Merrill, the best of colleagues, was equally receptive to the request for an afterword.

Susan McEachern, Rowman & Littlefield vice president and editorial director for international studies and a whirlwind of enthusiasm, efficiency, and professionalism, has been marvelous to work with. Series commander Mark Selden is surely the world's most alert and knowledgeable editor, and also came up with the title; the accomplished Mansi Bhatia gets credit for the subtitle. A young lady of keen eye and steady pencil, Margaret Kearney, produced the portraits. The indexer was Benjamin Darr.

For close scrutiny, slash-and-burn editing, redeeming encouragement, and a brilliant cover concept, plaudits to my mom, Nyna Brael Polumbaum.

My dad, photojournalist Ted Polumbaum, would have been delighted to see his picture of a Beijing Opera actor's Monkey King visage transmuted into a book cover; appreciation to the Newseum in Washington D.C., and especially to photo curator Karen Wyatt, for harboring my father's archives, including that photograph. Thanks as always to Gabriel Tianjiao Gao and Nathaniel Taihang Gao for their forbearance and precocious wisdom throughout their mother's academic career.

Finally, gratitude to the journalists who allowed themselves to be subjected to extended interrogations for this book, to my always delightful collaborator Xiong Lei, and to the countless other Chinese comrades and colleagues without whose enduring friendship, discerning guidance, and unwavering support this project never would have materialized. Responsibility for any errors of fact or interpretation is, of course, mine alone.

Index

About the Authors

Judy Polumbaum is a professor of journalism and mass communication at The University of Iowa in Iowa City, Iowa, USA.

Xiong Lei recently retired as a senior writer and top editor of Xinhua News Agency's China Features in Beijing. She continues to write on science and the environment. She and Polumbaum have been friends and colleagues since 1979.

Aryeh Neier (Foreword) is president of the Open Society Institute, based in New York City, and an adjunct professor of law at New York University. He previously served as executive director of Human Rights Watch and executive director of the American Civil Liberties Union.

Christopher Merrill (Afterword) directs the International Writing Program at The University of Iowa. A poet, prose writer, translator, and professor of English and comparative literature, he has authored four collections of poetry and four works of nonfiction.